Gourmet's
QUICK KITCHEN

Gourmet's QUICK KITCHEN

From the editors of Gourmet

PHOTOGRAPHS BY ROMULO A. YANES

Condé Nast Books
Random House
New York

Copyright © 1996 The Condé Nast Publications Inc.
All rights reserved under International and Pan-American
Copyright Conventions. Published in the United States by
Random House, Inc., New York, and simultaneously in Canada
by Random House of Canada Limited, Toronto.

LIBRARY OF CONGRESS
CATALOGING-IN-PUBLICATION DATA
Gourmet's quick kitchen: fast recipes, easy menus, and lighter
fare/from the editors of Gourmet; food photographs by
Romulo A. Yanes.
    p. cm.
    Includes index.
    ISBN 0-679-45257-5 (hc: alk. paper)
    1. Quick and easy cookery. 2. Menus. 3. Low-fat diet--
Recipes.   3. Low-calorie diet--Recipes. I. Gourmet.
TX833.5.G69 1996
641.5'55--dc2096-11079

Random House website address: http://www.randomhouse.com/

Some of the recipes in this work were published previously in
Gourmet Magazine.
Manufactured in the United States of America on acid-free paper

98765432
First Edition

All informative text in this book was written by
Diane Keitt and Caroline A. Schleifer.

FOR CONDÉ NAST BOOKS
Jill Cohen, *President*
Ellen Maria Bruzelius, *Direct Marketing Director*
Lucille Friedman, *Fulfillment Manager*
Tom Downing, *Direct Marketing Manager*
Jennifer Metz, *Direct Marketing Associate*
Diane Pesce, *Prepress Services Manager*
Serafino J. Cambareri, *Quality Control Manager*

FOR GOURMET BOOKS
Diane Keitt, *Director*
Caroline A. Schleifer, *Associate Editor*

FOR GOURMET MAGAZINE
Gail Zweigenthal, *Editor-in-Chief*

Zanne Early Stewart, *Executive Food Editor*
Kemp Miles Minifie, *Senior Food Editor*
Alexis M. Touchet, *Associate Food Editor*
Amy Mastrangelo, *Food Editor*
Lori Walther, *Food Editor*
Elizabeth Vought, *Food Editor*
Peggy Anderson, *Assistant Food Editor*

Romulo A. Yanes, *Photographer*
Marjorie H. Webb, *Style Director*
Nancy Purdum, *Senior Style Editor*

Produced in association with
MEDIA PROJECTS INCORPORATED
Carter Smith, *Executive Editor*
Anne B. Wright, *Project Editor*
John W. Kern, *Production Editor*
Marilyn Flaig, *Indexer*

BETH TONDREAU DESIGN, *Jacket and Book Design*
Agni Saucier, Illustrator

The text of this book was set in Meridien.
The four-color separations were done by
The Color Company, Seiple Lithographers, and
Applied Graphic Technologies. The book was printed
and bound at R. R. Donnelley and Sons. Stock is
Citation Webb Gloss, Westvaco.

Front Jacket: Jamaican-Spiced Pork Tenderloin, page 102; Sweet
Potato Purée, page 158; Black Bean and Roasted Vegetable Salad,
page 161. Back Jacket: Spiced Poached Pears, page 51. Menu
Opener (pages 10-11): Chilled Avocado Soup with Chili
Coriander Cream, page 74.

Acknowledgments

The editors of Gourmet Books would like to thank everyone who worked on *Gourmet's Quick Kitchen*, especially Leslie Pendleton, who developed over 100 new recipes and all the menus; and Alexis M. Touchet, Lori Walther, and Liz Vought, who created the new leaner/lighter recipes and tested (and retested) each new recipe. Also, we would like to give special thanks to Zanne Stewart, *Gourmet*'s Executive Food Editor, who found time this year to review every recipe, oversee every headnote, and get married!

Throughout the book you will enjoy outstanding food photographs by Romulo A. Yanes, styled by Marjorie Webb and Nancy Purdum. This successful team, along with food stylist Liz Vought, composed a picture-perfect book jacket.

The menus were enhanced with wine selections by Gerald Asher, *Gourmet*'s Wine Editor, and the manuscript was carefully polished with the help of Hobby McKenney, Anne Wright, John Kern, Karen Kern, Kim Horstman, and Angela Palmisono. Also, we would like to thank Judith Tropea for a clever book title, Agni Saucier for her lovely drawings, and Beth Tondreau for a fresh book design that illustrates the clean lines of today's quick kitchen.

All recipes in this book serve 2 and can be prepared in 45 minutes or less. Where indicated, recipes may be doubled to serve 4 which may require more preparation time and often larger bowls and pans.

Contents

THE RECIPES

Introduction

"This time, I'll keep it simple." How often have you invited a friend to dinner with this intention and then wondered what to serve? Our first "quick" cookbook, *Gourmet's In Short Order*, enabled me to treat my guests to special fare on my busiest days and to fix myself delicious meals and snacks on the run. Now, *Gourmet's Quick Kitchen* offers over 200 more outstanding recipes that combine nature's freshest ingredients without a lot of fuss. And, because we know how health conscious most of our readers have become, we've created over 40 delicious leaner/lighter recipes just for this book.

All the recipes in this volume were tested and retested in *Gourmet*'s kitchens until they passed the close scrutiny of our food editors. Outstanding flavor, quickness (each recipe can be prepared in 45 minutes or less), and ease of preparation were the main considerations. Twenty menus were composed and tested with the same strict requirements, and we made sure that there was plenty of variety.

Our leaner/lighter recipes are sprinkled throughout the chapters and identified by a feather symbol. We even offer a menu planner that combines many of these dishes (see pages 52-53). Currently, the FDA recommends a daily diet with no more than 30% of its calories coming from fat. These recipes and menus fit the bill and offer single-serving information such as calories, fat grams, and and percentage of calories from fat. For a well-balanced diet also include plenty of fresh fruits, vegetables, and whole grains.

A close look at our light recipes reveals cooking methods that emphasize flavor and minimize fat: oven broiling, outdoor grilling, sautéing in nonstick skillets, thickening sauces with vegetables, marinating foods without fat, and boosting flavors with piquant vinegars and fresh fruit juices are just a few of our tips that make a difference.

With *Gourmet's Quick Kitchen* you will not only cook faster, you will eat better. We think you'll agree, the term "fast food" is now even more appealing.

> **KEY TO THE RECIPES:**
> *All recipes in this book serve 2; many may be doubled to serve 4*

GAIL ZWEIGENTHAL
Editor-in-Chief

Individual Chocolate Soufflés (page 173)

THE
MENUS

An Alfresco Spring Brunch

APRICOT WINE SPRITZERS

SPINACH, RED PEPPER,
AND FETA QUICHE

ROMAINE SALAD WITH
RADISHES, OLIVES, AND MINT

FROZEN YOGURT WITH
RASPBERRY PORT SAUCE

Serves 2

Spinach, Red Pepper, and Feta Quiche;
Romaine Salad with Radishes, Olives, and Mint

An Alfresco Spring Brunch

Although our brunch can be enjoyed at any time of the year, it has just the sparkle needed to celebrate spring. If you'd like to serve 4, simply make two quiches and double the remaining recipes. Be sure to have unopened bottles of seltzer or club soda on hand for spritzers with plenty of fizz.

QUICK TIPS:
- Pre-washed packaged spinach may be used for the quiche filling.
- 1 packaged pie dough round may be used for the quiche shell.

APRICOT WINE SPRITZERS

⅔ cup dry white wine
½ cup canned apricot nectar
½ cup fresh seltzer or club soda

Garnish: 2 lime slices

Divide wine and nectar between 2 large wineglasses and stir mixture. Add ice. Top each drink with seltzer or club soda and stir. Garnish spritzers with lime slices. Makes 2 drinks. May be doubled.

SPINACH, RED PEPPER, AND FETA QUICHE

For pastry shell
⅓ cup plus 3 tablespoons all-purpose flour
3 tablespoons cold unsalted butter
1 tablespoon cold vegetable shortening
1½ tablespoons ice water plus additional if necessary

For filling
1 tablespoon olive oil
½ medium red bell pepper, cut into thin strips (about ⅓ cup)
2 cups packed fresh spinach, coarse stems discarded and leaves washed well and spun dry (about 5 ounces)
2 large eggs
⅓ cup heavy cream or milk
⅓ cup crumbled feta

Preheat oven to 425° F.
Make pastry shell:
In a bowl with a pastry blender or in a small food processor blend or pulse together flour, butter, shortening, and a pinch salt until mixture resembles coarse meal. Add 1½ tablespoons ice water and toss with a fork or pulse until water is incorporated. Add enough additional ice water, 1 teaspoon at a time, tossing or pulsing to incorporate, until mixture begins to form a dough. Pat dough onto bottom and ½ inch up side of a 7½-inch tart pan with a removable fluted rim or a 9-inch pie plate and bake in lower third of oven until set and pale golden, about 7 minutes.

Make filling while shell is baking:

In a large skillet heat oil over moderately high heat until hot but not smoking and sauté bell pepper, stirring, 1 minute. Add spinach and sauté, stirring, until wilted and tender, about 1 minute. Remove skillet from heat and season vegetables with salt and pepper. In a small bowl whisk together eggs and cream or milk. Sprinkle feta in bottom of shell and spread vegetables over it. Pour egg mixture over vegetables.

Bake quiche on a baking sheet in middle of oven 15 minutes. Reduce oven temperature to 350° F. and bake quiche until set, about 10 minutes more. Serves 2.

Photo on page 12

ROMAINE SALAD WITH RADISHES, OLIVES, AND MINT

½ small garlic clove, minced and mashed to a paste with a pinch salt
1 teaspoon fresh lemon juice
1 tablespoon olive oil
1 head romaine, small inner leaves only, washed well and spun dry
4 Kalamata or other brine-cured black olives, pitted and sliced
3 radishes, sliced thin crosswise
1 teaspoon julienne strips of fresh mint leaves

In a large bowl whisk together garlic paste, lemon juice, and oil until combined well. Add remaining ingredients and toss well. Serves 2. May be doubled.

Photo on page 12

FROZEN YOGURT WITH RASPBERRY PORT SAUCE

1 cup fresh raspberries (about 6 ounces)
2 tablespoons sugar
2 tablespoons Tawny Port
1 tablespoon fresh lemon juice
4 scoops peach or vanilla frozen yogurt (about ½ pint)

In a blender or food processor purée raspberries with sugar, Port, and lemon juice until smooth and force through a fine sieve into a bowl.

Scoop frozen yogurt into 2 stemmed glasses and top with sauce. Serves 2. May be doubled.

Carefree Pasta Lunch

PASTA WITH
PROSCIUTTO, PEPPERS, AND HERBS

GARLIC BREAD

ARUGULA OR MIXED GREEN SALAD

APRICOT YOGURT MOUSSE

*Serves 2
(All recipes may be
doubled to serve 4)*

DUCKHORN VINEYARDS
NAPA VALLEY
SAUVIGNON BLANC
1994

Carefree Pasta Lunch

B usy lifestyles call for carefree meals, and although our pasta lunch can be made in a flash, it has special touches. For example, our pasta dish calls for gigli del gargano (ruffle-edged, cone-shaped pasta), prosciutto, and fresh herbs. For full flavor, always cut fresh herbs just before adding them to the finished dish.

QUICK TIP:
- Be sure to use a metal bowl set in a larger bowl of ice and cold water when cooling the dessert's apricot mixture, as it will chill the mixture more quickly. Also, stir the mixture frequently to cool faster.

PASTA WITH PROSCIUTTO, PEPPERS, AND HERBS

- ½ pound *gigli del gargano* (ruffle-edged, cone-shaped pasta) or *rotini* (spiral pasta)
- 1 small red onion, chopped fine
- 1 yellow bell pepper, chopped fine
- 3 tablespoons extra-virgin olive oil
- 1 7-ounce jar roasted red peppers, drained and chopped fine
- ¾ cup finely chopped prosciutto or other ham (about 3 ounces)
- 1 cup packed mixed fresh herbs such as basil, mint, and parsley leaves, washed well, spun dry, and chopped fine

Accompaniments: lemon wedges and freshly grated Parmesan

Bring a 3½-quart saucepan filled with 2 quarts salted water to a boil for pasta.

In a heavy skillet cook onion and yellow pepper in 1 tablespoon oil over moderately low heat, stirring, until softened and stir in red peppers and ham. Cook pasta in boiling water until *al dente* and drain well. In a bowl toss pasta with pepper mixture, remaining 2 tablespoons oil, herbs, and salt and pepper to taste.

Serve pasta with lemon and Parmesan. Serves 2. May be doubled.

Photo on page 16

GARLIC BREAD

1   6- to 8-inch piece Italian bread, halved horizontally
1   large garlic clove
2   tablespoons unsalted butter, softened
⅛   teaspoon salt
¼   teaspoon paprika

Preheat broiler.

Arrange bread, cut sides down, on a baking sheet and broil about 4 inches from heat until crust is crisp, about 1 minute.

Force garlic through a garlic press into a small bowl and stir in butter, salt, and pepper to taste. Spread mixture on cut sides of bread and arrange, cut sides up, on baking sheet. Sprinkle bread with paprika and broil about 4 inches from heat until golden, about 2 minutes. Sandwich bread halves together and cut crosswise into 4 slices. Serves 2 generously. May be doubled.

APRICOT YOGURT MOUSSE

½   teaspoon unflavored gelatin
⅔   cup cold water
⅓   cup dried apricots
¼   cup sugar
½   teaspoon vanilla
½   cup plain yogurt
⅓   cup well-chilled heavy cream

In a cup sprinkle gelatin over ⅓ cup cold water and let soften. In a small saucepan simmer apricots, sugar, and remaining ⅓ cup water, covered, 15 minutes. Stir in gelatin mixture and simmer, stirring, until gelatin is dissolved. In a blender purée apricot mixture with vanilla and transfer to a metal bowl set in a larger bowl of ice and cold water. Stir purée until cold and whisk in yogurt. In a chilled bowl beat cream until it just holds stiff peaks and fold into yogurt mixture gently but thoroughly.

Divide mousse between 2 small bowls and chill until ready to serve. Serves 2. May be doubled.

Lunch by the Fire

LEEK, POTATO, AND
SAUSAGE SOUP

CARAWAY BROWN BREAD

GREEN SALAD

DOUBLE-CHOCOLATE
PEANUT BUTTER COOKIES

Serves 2
(All recipes may be
doubled to serve 4)

PARDUCCI
MENDOCINO
PETITE SIRAH
1992

Lunch by the Fire

TECHNIQUE TIP:
- *The interaction of buttermilk, molasses, and baking soda causes our brown bread to rise, so shape the dough quickly into loaves and bake immediately.*

LEEK, POTATO, AND SAUSAGE SOUP

- $\frac{1}{4}$ teaspoon cumin seeds
- $\frac{1}{4}$ teaspoon caraway seeds
- 1 medium leek (white part only), halved lengthwise, sliced thin crosswise, washed well, and drained (about $1\frac{1}{4}$ cups)
- 1 tablespoon unsalted butter
- 2 cups low-salt chicken broth
- 1 small boiling potato (about $\frac{1}{4}$ pound), cut into $\frac{1}{2}$-inch cubes
- $\frac{1}{4}$ pound *kielbasa*, cut crosswise into $\frac{1}{4}$-inch-thick slices, and slices quartered
- 1 tablespoon heavy cream
- $\frac{1}{4}$ cup thinly sliced well-washed fresh spinach leaves

In a dry heavy saucepan toast cumin and caraway seeds over moderate heat, stirring, 2 minutes, or until very fragrant, and transfer to a plate. In pan cook leek in butter, stirring occasionally, 5 minutes, or until very soft, and stir in broth and potato. Bring broth to a boil and simmer 10 minutes, or until potato is tender. Stir in toasted seeds, *kielbasa*, cream, and salt and pepper to taste and simmer 5 minutes.

Just before serving, stir in spinach. Serves 2. May be doubled.

Photo on page 20

CARAWAY BROWN BREAD

  2 cups whole-wheat flour plus
      additional for dusting loaves
  1 teaspoon baking soda
  1 teaspoon salt
  1 cup buttermilk
  1 tablespoon molasses
 ½ teaspoon caraway seeds

Preheat oven to 375° F. and grease a baking sheet.

    In a large bowl whisk together 2 cups whole-wheat flour, baking soda, and salt. Add buttermilk, molasses, and caraway, stirring until a dough forms. With floured hands halve dough and form halves into round loaves. Put loaves on baking sheet and dust tops with additional flour.

    Cut a shallow "X" (2 inches wide) on top of each loaf and bake in middle of oven 25 minutes, or until lightly browned. Cool loaves on a rack. Makes two 4-inch loaves. May be doubled.

DOUBLE-CHOCOLATE PEANUT BUTTER COOKIES

 ½ stick (¼ cup) unsalted butter,
      softened
 ½ cup sugar
 ¼ cup chunky-style peanut butter
  1 large egg
 ½ cup all-purpose flour
 ¼ cup unsweetened cocoa powder
 ¼ teaspoon baking soda
 ¼ teaspoon salt
 ½ cup semisweet chocolate chips

Preheat oven to 350° F.

    In a bowl with an electric mixer beat together butter, sugar, and peanut butter until light and fluffy and beat in egg until smooth. Into mixture sift together flour, cocoa powder, baking soda, and salt, beating until just combined well. Stir in chocolate chips until evenly distributed.

    Drop cookie dough by heaping teaspoons about 1 inch apart on an ungreased large baking sheet and bake in middle of oven 10 minutes, or until just firm to the touch. Transfer cookies with a metal spatula to racks to cool. Makes about 34 cookies. May be doubled.

A Lazy Day Summer Lunch

STEAK SALAD WITH
PICKLED VEGETABLES

CRUSTY BREAD
(STORE-BOUGHT)

CINNAMON SHORTCAKES WITH
PEACHES AND CREAM

Serves 2
(All recipes may be
doubled to serve 4)

COLUMBIA CREST
WASHINGTON STATE
GAMAY BEAUJOLAIS
1994

A Lazy Day Summer Lunch

When the hazy, hot, humid days of summer are upon us, you'll want to cut corners in the kitchen with leftovers in our luscious lazy day lunch. Earlier in the week simply throw an extra steak on the grill for our steak salad. Slice the meat just before tossing it with pickled vegetables and aromatic seasonings. Our dessert boasts crumbly cinnamon shortcakes (be sure to use a serrated knife to halve them) and summer's best ripe peaches.

QUICK TIP:
- For dessert, the macerated peaches may be spooned over ice cream, frozen yogurt, or bakery-bought shortcakes or pound cake. (This also will keep your kitchen cool on a hot day.)

STEAK SALAD WITH PICKLED VEGETABLES

1 pound leftover cooked steak, sliced thin
1 celery rib, sliced thin diagonally
1 cup drained bottled *giardiniera* (assorted pickled vegetables), chopped if desired
¼ cup chopped drained bottled roasted red peppers
¼ cup chopped fresh flat-leafed parsley leaves
2 tablespoons olive oil
1 teaspoon Worcestershire sauce, or to taste
½ head red-leaf lettuce for lining plates

In a large bowl toss together all ingredients except lettuce and season with salt and pepper.

Line 2 plates with lettuce and mound steak salad on top. Serves 2 generously. May be doubled.

Photo on page 24

CINNAMON SHORTCAKES WITH PEACHES AND CREAM

    2 very ripe peeled and pitted peaches
        or 4 canned peach halves
    2 tablespoons granulated sugar
    1 tablespoon peach schnapps
        if desired
  $\frac{1}{4}$ teaspoon vanilla

For biscuits

  $\frac{1}{2}$ cup all-purpose flour
  $\frac{3}{4}$ teaspoon baking powder
  $\frac{3}{4}$ teaspoon cinnamon
  $\frac{1}{8}$ teaspoon salt
    1 tablespoon firmly packed
        brown sugar
    2 tablespoons cold unsalted butter,
        cut into bits
    3 tablespoons milk
    1 teaspoon granulated sugar

  $\frac{1}{3}$ cup well-chilled heavy cream
    1 tablespoon confectioners' sugar

Preheat oven to 400° F. and butter a baking sheet.

Cut peaches into $\frac{1}{2}$-inch cubes. In a bowl combine half of peaches with sugar, schnapps, and vanilla, mashing lightly with a fork, and stir in remaining peaches. Let peaches macerate while making biscuits.

Make biscuits:

In a bowl whisk together flour, baking powder, $\frac{1}{2}$ teaspoon cinnamon, and salt and add brown sugar and butter. With fingertips blend mixture until it resembles coarse meal and stir in milk until a dough forms. In a cup stir together granulated sugar and remaining $\frac{1}{4}$ teaspoon cinnamon. Drop dough in 2 mounds on baking sheet and sprinkle tops with cinnamon sugar. Bake biscuits in middle of oven 15 minutes, or until golden. Transfer biscuits carefully to a rack and cool.

In a chilled bowl beat cream with confectioners' sugar until it holds stiff peaks. Cut off top fourth of biscuit carefully with a serrated knife (it will be very crumbly), putting bottoms onto 2 small plates and reserving tops. Spoon peaches with liquid over biscuit bottoms and top with whipped cream. Cover cream with reserved tops. Serves 2. May be doubled.

Barbecue for a Special Occasion

SWORDFISH, BACON, AND
CHERRY TOMATO KEBABS

SAUTÉED SPINACH CHIFFONADE
WITH SHALLOTS

HERBED RICE SALAD

LEMON POPPY SEED COOKIES

BERRY SORBET
(STORE-BOUGHT)

Serves 2

LOCKWOOD
MONTEREY
CHARDONNAY
1993

Swordfish, Bacon, and Cherry Tomato Kebabs;
Sautéed Spinach Chiffonade with Shallots

Barbecue for a Special Occasion

For an informal yet special easy menu rely on our barbecue. The kebabs and spinach chiffonade take only a few minutes to cook after the rice salad is tossed, allowing maximum time to spend with your guests. In choosing swordfish for the kebabs, avoid steaks with brown meat which has an oilier taste. For the chiffonade, choose large-leafed spinach which will be easier to cut. Flat-leafed parsley will give more flavor to the rice salad than the curly variety.

QUICK TIP:
- *As with many buttery cookie doughs, our poppy-seed dough is chilled briefly for easier handling. Flatten the dough to speed up chilling time.*

SWORDFISH, BACON, AND CHERRY TOMATO KEBABS

- ¾ pound swordfish steak (about ½ inch thick), cut into 1-inch cubes
- 1 large garlic clove, minced
- 2 teaspoons fresh lemon juice
- 2 teaspoons olive oil
- 8 slices bacon
- 12 vine-ripened cherry tomatoes

Accompaniment: lemon wedges

Prepare grill.

In a shallow dish toss swordfish with garlic, lemon juice, and oil to coat and marinate, covered and chilled, 20 minutes.

In a large skillet cook bacon over moderate heat until pale golden but still soft and transfer to paper towels to drain, reserving drippings.

Onto four 10-inch skewers thread alternately swordfish, bacon folded in thirds, and tomatoes. Brush kebabs with some reserved drippings and grill on an oiled rack set 5 to 6 inches over glowing coals until swordfish is just cooked through, about 3 to 4 minutes on each side.

Serve fish kebabs with lemon wedges. Serves 2. May be doubled.

Photo on page 28

SAUTÉED SPINACH CHIFFONADE WITH SHALLOTS

- ¾ pound fresh spinach, stems discarded and leaves washed well and spun dry (about 1 bunch)
- 2 large shallots, minced
- 2 tablespoons olive oil

Working in batches, stack spinach leaves and cut into ½-inch-wide strips. In a large heavy skillet cook shallots in oil over moderate heat, stirring, until softened. Add spinach and salt and pepper to taste and sauté over moderately high heat, stirring, until wilted and tender, about 3 minutes. Serves 2. May be doubled.

Photo on page 28

HERBED RICE SALAD

1⅓ cups water
3 tablespoons olive oil
½ teaspoon salt
⅔ cup long-grain white rice
2 teaspoons mustard seeds
⅔ cup packed fresh parsley leaves,
washed well, spun dry, and minced
1½ teaspoons minced fresh
tarragon leaves, or to taste
¼ cup minced red onion
1½ tablespoons white-wine vinegar

In a heavy saucepan bring water to a boil with 1 tablespoon oil and salt and stir in rice and mustard seeds. Cook rice over low heat, covered, 20 minutes, or until rice is tender and water is absorbed. Fluff rice with a fork and transfer to a heatproof bowl. Cool rice, tossing occasionally, 10 minutes. Stir in remaining 2 tablespoons oil, remaining ingredients, and salt and pepper to taste and toss well. Serves 2. May be doubled.

LEMON POPPY SEED COOKIES

¾ stick (6 tablespoons) unsalted
butter, softened
½ cup sugar
½ teaspoon vanilla
1½ teaspoons freshly grated lemon zest
2 tablespoons fresh lemon juice
¾ cup all-purpose flour
½ teaspoon baking powder
¼ teaspoon baking soda
⅛ teaspoon salt
1 tablespoon poppy seeds

Accompaniment: berry sorbet

Preheat oven to 350° F.

In a bowl with an electric mixer beat together butter and sugar and add vanilla, zest, and lemon juice, beating until smooth. Into mixture sift together flour, baking powder, baking soda, and salt and add poppy seeds, beating dough until just combined well. Wrap dough in plastic wrap and flatten ½-inch-thick. Freeze dough 10 minutes to firm it.

Drop dough by rounded teaspoons about 2 inches apart onto 2 ungreased baking sheets. Bake cookies in upper and lower thirds of oven, switching sheets halfway through baking, 8 minutes, or until edges are just golden. Transfer cookies with a metal spatula to racks to cool.

Serve cookies with sorbet. Makes about 24 cookies.

A Festive Summer Dinner

BRUSCHETTA WITH TOMATO,
BLACK BEANS, AND ARUGULA

VEGETABLE TORTILLA LASAGNE

COCONUT CHEESECAKES WITH
PINEAPPLE COMPOTE

Serves 2

CONDE DE VALDEMAR
RIOJA RESERVA
1990

A Festive Summer Dinner

W*hether you're celebrating a birthday, a promotion, or just a beautiful summer evening, our dinner combines the zesty flavors of Mexico and Italy and evokes the festive feelings of sunny climes. This menu requires a bit of organization: The coconut cheesecakes, though quick to prepare, need some chilling time, so make them first. Assemble the tortilla lasagne next, up to the baking stage. While enjoying the bruschetta, bake the lasagne.*

QUICK TIP:
- *Buy graham cracker crumbs or crush crackers in a blender for speedy cheesecake crusts.*

BRUSCHETTA WITH TOMATO, BLACK BEANS, AND ARUGULA

½ cup rinsed drained canned
  black beans
1 vine-ripened tomato, seeded and
  cut into ¼-inch dice
¼ cup well-washed shredded
  arugula leaves
1 teaspoon red-wine vinegar
¼ teaspoon sugar
6 ⅓-inch-thick slices Italian bread
1 tablespoon olive oil
  (preferably extra-virgin)
1 garlic clove

Preheat oven to 500° F.

Finely chop ¼ cup beans and in a bowl stir together with whole beans, tomato, arugula, vinegar, sugar, and salt and pepper to taste.

On a baking sheet arrange bread slices in one layer and toast in upper third of oven 4 minutes, or until golden. While toasts are warm, brush both sides with oil and rub one side with garlic. Top toasts with bean mixture. Makes 6 hors d'oeuvres, serving 2. May be doubled.

VEGETABLE TORTILLA LASAGNE

You'll have leftover tortilla pieces from making the lasagne—brush them lightly with oil, dust with chili powder, cut into strips, and toast lightly for a snack that's delicious with a frozen margarita.

1 large zucchini (about 10 ounces),
  cut crosswise into ¼-inch-thick
  slices
¾ cup corn (thawed if frozen)
¼ cup ricotta
1¼ cups grated Monterey Jack
  (about ¼ pound)
½ teaspoon ground cumin seeds
1 cup tomato salsa (about 9 ounces)
6 6-inch corn tortillas
1 7-ounce jar roasted red peppers,
  drained and patted dry
3 tablespoons chopped fresh
  coriander sprigs

Accompaniment: lime wedges

Preheat oven to 500° F. and grease 2 shallow baking pans and a loaf pan, 8½ by 4½ by 3 inches.

Arrange zucchini in one layer in first baking pan and in half of second baking pan. Spread corn in remaining half of second pan. Season zucchini and corn with salt and pepper and roast in upper and lower thirds of oven, stirring corn and switching position of pans halfway through roasting, about 10 minutes, or until lightly browned.

While vegetables are roasting, in a small bowl stir together ricotta, 1 cup Monterey Jack, cumin, and salt and pepper to taste. Drain salsa in a fine sieve set over a bowl 3 seconds (do not press on solids) and transfer to another bowl.

Trim tortillas with scissors into six 5-by 3¾-inch rectangles. Arrange 2 rectangles in bottom of loaf pan, overlapping in middle. Spread ¼ cup salsa over tortillas and top with half of ricotta mixture, half of zucchini, half of peppers, half of corn, and 1 tablespoon coriander. Repeat layering with tortilla rectangles, ¼ cup salsa, remaining ricotta mixture, remaining vegetables, and 1 tablespoon coriander in same manner. Top with remaining 2 tortilla rectangles, remaining ½ cup salsa, remaining ¼ cup Monterey Jack, and remaining tablespoon coriander. Cover lasagne with foil and bake in middle of oven 12 minutes, or until heated through and cheese is melted. Let lasagne stand, covered, 5 minutes before serving.

Cut lasagne in half and serve with lime wedges. Serves 2.

Photo on page 32

COCONUT CHEESECAKES WITH PINEAPPLE COMPOTE

1 tablespoon unsalted butter
¼ cup graham cracker crumbs
¾ cup cream cheese, softened
¼ cup granulated sugar
½ teaspoon coconut extract
1 large egg
¾ cup canned chopped pineapple, drained well
2 tablespoons firmly packed light brown sugar
¼ teaspoon fresh lemon juice, or to taste

Preheat oven to 350° F.

In a small saucepan melt butter over moderate heat and stir in cracker crumbs. Divide crumb mixture between two 1-cup ramekins (4 inches in diameter) and press onto bottoms to form crusts. Bake crusts in middle of oven 5 minutes and cool on a rack 5 minutes.

While crusts are cooling, in a bowl with an electric mixer beat together cream cheese, granulated sugar, extract, and a pinch salt until combined well. Beat in egg until combined well and divide filling between ramekins. Bake cheesecakes in middle of oven 20 minutes, or until just set.

While cheesecakes are baking, in a small heavy saucepan simmer pineapple, brown sugar, and a pinch salt, stirring, until sugar is dissolved and stir in lemon juice.

Cool cheesecakes on a rack 5 minutes and chill 10 minutes, or until ready to serve.

Run a knife around cheesecakes and invert onto 2 plates. Spoon pineapple compote around cheesecakes. Makes two 4-inch cheesecakes, serving 2.

A Hearty
Bachelor's Dinner

STEAK AU POIVRE

SPINACH WITH PERNOD

TURNIPS WITH BREAD CRUMBS
AND PARSLEY

BUTTERSCOTCH CHOCOLATE CHIP
BREAD PUDDING

Serves 2

ESTANCIA
ALEXANDER VALLEY
SANGIOVESE
1993

Steak au Poivre; Spinach with Pernod; and
Turnips with Bread Crumbs and Parsley

A Hearty Bachelor's Dinner

Anyone with a hearty appetite will enjoy this French bistro-style dinner. Instead of french fries, surprise guests with tender turnips. For the sweetest flavor, look for small white ones with rosy tops. Feel free to substitute your favorite cut of beef in the steak au poivre recipe, but choose a flavorful one (such as sirloin or porterhouse) to hold up to the powerful peppercorn coating. We suggest using day-old baguette for the best bread pudding, but be sure to cut it up before it becomes stale, or it will crumble.

TECHNIQUE TIP:
- To crush spices without scattering them, roll a dish towel into a collar on your work surface. Put the spices in the center and crush with the bottom of a heavy skillet.

STEAK AU POIVRE

1 tablespoon whole black peppercorns
1 teaspoon whole white peppercorns
1 teaspoon dried green peppercorns
1 teaspoon fennel seeds
2 ¾-pound boneless shell steaks (about 1¼ inches thick)
1 tablespoon unsalted butter
1 tablespoon vegetable oil
3 tablespoons heavy cream
2 tablespoons Cognac or other brandy

In a heavy-duty sealable plastic bag or between 2 sheets wax paper coarsely crush peppercorns and fennel seeds with bottom of a heavy skillet. Pat steaks dry and coat both sides with peppercorn mixture. In a 10-inch heavy skillet heat butter and oil over moderate heat until hot but not smoking and cook steaks 4 to 5 minutes on each side for medium-rare. Season steaks with salt and transfer to heated plates.

Pour off excess fat from skillet and add cream and brandy. Boil mixture, scraping up browned bits, until sauce thickens enough to coat back of spoon, about 1 minute, and season with salt. Spoon sauce over steaks. Serves 2 generously.

Photo on page 36

SPINACH WITH PERNOD

4 shallots, minced
2 garlic cloves, minced
2 tablespoons unsalted butter
2 bunches spinach (about 2 pounds), stems discarded and leaves washed well and drained in a colander
1 teaspoon Pernod or other anise-flavored liqueur

In a deep 12-inch skillet cook shallots and garlic in butter over moderate heat until softened, about 2 minutes. Add spinach with any water clinging to leaves and cook, turning constantly with tongs, until wilted and liquid is evaporated, about 4 minutes. Season spinach with salt and pepper and drizzle with Pernod. Cook spinach, turning, 2 minutes. Serves 2. May be doubled.

Photo on page 36

Turnips with Bread Crumbs and Parsley

4 small turnips (about ¾ pound), peeled
1 tablespoon unsalted butter
2 tablespoons fresh bread crumbs
2 teaspoons minced fresh parsley leaves
½ teaspoon freshly grated lemon zest

In a large saucepan of boiling salted water cook turnips 15 minutes and drain. When turnips are cool enough to handle, cut each into 8 wedges.

In a large skillet cook turnips in butter over moderate heat, stirring occasionally, until almost tender and golden on the edges, about 10 minutes. Stir in bread crumbs, parsley, zest, and salt and pepper to taste and cook, stirring occasionally, until turnips are tender, about 5 minutes. Serves 2. May be doubled.

Photo on page 36

Butterscotch Chocolate Chip Bread Pudding

2 tablespoons unsalted butter, melted
2 cups ¾-inch cubes French bread (about ½ loaf)
1 large egg
½ teaspoon vanilla
¼ teaspoon salt
⅓ cup plus 1 tablespoon firmly packed brown sugar
1¼ cups milk
2 tablespoons semisweet chocolate chips

Accompaniment: vanilla ice cream

Preheat oven to 350° F. and butter a loaf pan, 9 by 5 by 3 inches.

In a bowl drizzle butter on bread. In another bowl whisk together egg, vanilla, salt, and ⅓ cup brown sugar. In a small heavy saucepan heat milk just to a boil and add to egg mixture in a stream, whisking. Pour custard over bread, stirring to combine well, and let stand 5 minutes. Stir in chocolate chips and turn mixture into loaf pan. Sprinkle pudding with remaining tablespoon brown sugar and bake in middle of oven 25 minutes, or until a knife inserted in center comes out clean.

Serve pudding warm with ice cream. Serves 2. May be doubled.

An Elegant Asian Dinner

SESAME NOODLES WITH
CUCUMBER

PAN-SEARED RED SNAPPER
IN GINGER BROTH

SOURDOUGH ROLLS
(STORE-BOUGHT)

ALMOND GALETTE WITH
FRESH FRUIT AND WHIPPED CREAM

Serves 2

DR. LOOSEN
ERDENER TREPPCHEN
RIESLING KABINETT
1994

Pan-Seared Red Snapper in Ginger Broth

An Elegant Asian Dinner

This East-meets-West meal balances hearty sesame noodles with delicate snapper in a fragrant ginger-infused broth, and a warm, buttery dessert. The galette, usually a French confection, is reminiscent of Chinese almond cookies, and is delicious served with jasmine or chrysanthemum tea.

TECHNIQUE TIPS:
- For bok choy, stack the leaves, cut off the green parts and shred them, then cut the white stalks crosswise.
- To ensure tender julienned gingerroot, peel a section of root, slice quarter-sized pieces crosswise against the grain to break the fibers, then cut each slice into slivers.

SESAME NOODLES WITH CUCUMBER

  2 ounces *linguine*
  1 small garlic clove, minced
  1 tablespoon well-stirred *tahini* (sesame seed paste)
  1 scallion, sliced thin
2½ teaspoons fresh lemon juice
1½ teaspoons soy sauce
  1 tablespoon minced fresh parsley leaves
 ½ teaspoon honey
  1 pinch cayenne
  1 tablespoon water plus additional if necessary
 ¼ cup peeled seeded chopped cucumber
  1 tablespoon chopped unsalted peanuts

In a saucepan bring salted water to a boil for *linguine*.

In a bowl stir together garlic, *tahini*, scallion, lemon juice, soy sauce, parsley, honey, cayenne, 1 tablespoon water, and salt to taste until combined well.

Cook *linguine* in boiling water until tender and drain in a colander. Rinse *linguine* briefly. Add *linguine* to *tahini* sauce with cucumber and toss, adding additional water if necessary to thin sauce.

Divide noodles between 2 plates and sprinkle with peanuts. Serves 2. May be doubled.

PAN-SEARED RED SNAPPER IN GINGER BROTH

 ½ *bok choy* (about ¼ pound)
  2 teaspoons vegetable oil
  2 teaspoons Asian sesame oil
  1 carrot, scored lengthwise and sliced thin crosswise
  1 1½-inch-long piece peeled fresh gingerroot, cut into fine julienne strips (about ¼ cup)
  2 tablespoons Scotch
  2 cups low-salt chicken broth
  1 teaspoon sugar
  2 scallions, cut into 2-inch julienne strips
  2 small red snapper or other white fish fillets with skin (4 to 5 ounces each)

½ teaspoon cornstarch
½ teaspoon curry powder

Garnish: fresh coriander sprigs

Cut leaves from *bok choy* stalks. Slice leaves thin and cut stalks diagonally into ½-inch-thick slices. In a large heavy saucepan heat 1 teaspoon of each oil over moderately high heat until hot but not smoking and stir-fry bok choy stalks, carrot, and gingerroot 1 minute. Add Scotch, broth, and sugar and simmer, covered, 5 minutes. Add *bok choy* leaves and scallions and simmer, covered, 3 minutes, or until tender. Season broth with salt and pepper and keep warm, uncovered.

Pat fish dry and rub cornstarch and curry powder into skin. Halve each fillet diagonally. In a 9-inch non-stick skillet heat remaining 2 teaspoons vegetable and sesame oils together over moderately high heat until hot but not smoking and sauté fish, skin sides down and flattening occasionally with a metal spatula, until golden, about 2 minutes. Turn fish and sauté until just cooked through, about 2 minutes more.

Divide broth between 2 bowls and top with fish, skin sides up. Garnish each serving with coriander sprigs. Serves 2. May be doubled.

Photo on page 40

ALMOND GALETTE WITH FRESH FRUIT AND WHIPPED CREAM

½ stick (¼ cup) unsalted butter, softened
½ cup plus 1 tablespoon sugar
1 large egg
¼ teaspoon almond extract
½ cup all-purpose flour
¼ cup sliced almonds, ground fine in a small food processor
½ teaspoon baking powder
¼ teaspoon salt

Accompaniments: mixed berries or other fresh fruit and whipped cream

Preheat oven to 350° F.

In a bowl with an electric mixer beat butter with ½ cup sugar until light and fluffy and beat in egg and extract until smooth. In another bowl whisk together flour, almonds, baking powder, and salt. Add flour mixture to butter mixture and beat until dough is just combined. Spoon dough into an 8-inch round cake pan, smoothing top, and sprinkle with remaining tablespoon sugar. Bake galette in middle of oven 15 minutes, or until golden.

Serve galette warm with fruit and whipped cream. Serves 2 to 4.

Dinner for a Snowy Eve

BUTTERNUT SQUASH AND
APPLE SOUP WITH BACON

CHEDDAR CHUTNEY TOASTS

WURST AND SAUERKRAUT PAPRIKA

BOILED NEW POTATOES

CARAMEL PEAR FOOL

Serves 2
(All recipes may be
doubled to serve 4)

PONZI
WILLAMETTE VALLEY
PINOT GRIS
1994

Butternut Squash and Apple Soup
with Bacon; Cheddar Chutney Toasts

Dinner for a Snowy Eve

After a day of skiing, sledding, or just playing in the snow, nothing warms you up like a comforting soup and a filling casserole. For the wurst and sauerkraut paprika, make sure to use vacuum-sealed packages of sauerkraut from the refrigerator section of your supermarket (avoid canned). For an intense caramel flavor in our pear fool, cook the sugar to a deep amber color, taking care not to burn it. As soon as it's dark enough, carefully stir in the liquid ingredients to stop the sugar from cooking.

QUICK TIP:
• If you're rushed, you can often find peeled butternut squash in the produce section of your supermarket.

BUTTERNUT SQUASH AND APPLE SOUP WITH BACON

2 slices bacon, chopped coarse
½ medium onion, chopped fine (about ½ cup)
1 large leek, white and pale green parts chopped fine and washed well (about 1 cup)
1 large garlic clove, minced
½ bay leaf
1¼ pounds butternut squash, seeded, peeled, and cut into 1-inch pieces (about 3 cups)
1 medium Granny Smith or other tart apple
2 cups low-salt chicken broth
½ cup water plus additional for thinning soup
2 tablespoons *crème fraîche* or sour cream

Accompaniments: crème fraîche or sour cream, chopped unpeeled apple, and Cheddar chutney toasts (recipe follows)

In a heavy saucepan cook bacon over moderate heat, stirring occasionally, until crisp and transfer with a slotted spoon to paper towels to drain. Pour off all but 1½ tablespoons drippings. In drippings remaining in pan cook onion, leek, and garlic with bay leaf and salt and pepper to taste over moderate heat, stirring, until vegetables are softened. Peel and chop apple. To vegetables add squash, apple, broth, and ½ cup water and simmer, covered, until squash is very tender, about 15 minutes. Discard bay leaf.

In a blender purée mixture in batches, transferring to another saucepan, and stir in enough additional water to thin soup to desired consistency.

Whisk in *crème fraîche* or sour cream and salt and pepper to taste and heat soup over moderately low heat until hot (do not boil).

Serve soup, topped with bacon, *crème fraîche* or sour cream, and apple, with toasts. Makes about 4½ cups, serving 2. May be doubled.

Photo on page 44

Cheddar Chutney Toasts

6 ¾-inch-thick diagonal slices
   Italian or French bread
2 tablespoons Major Grey's chutney,
   large pieces chopped
1½ teaspoons Dijon mustard
¾ cup grated extra-sharp Cheddar

Preheat broiler.

On a baking sheet arrange bread in one layer and broil about 4 inches from heat until golden, 1 to 2 minutes on each side.

In a small bowl stir together chutney and mustard and spread on one side of each toast. Divide Cheddar among toasts and broil about 4 inches from heat until cheese is melted and golden, 2 to 3 minutes. Makes 6 toasts. May be doubled.

Photo on page 44

Wurst and Sauerkraut Paprika

1 large onion, sliced thin
2 tablespoons unsalted butter
1 pound packaged sauerkraut,
   rinsed well and drained well
1¼ cups chicken broth or water
2 tablespoons raisins
1 tablespoon Dijon mustard
2 teaspoons paprika
¾ teaspoon caraway seeds if desired
1¼ pounds German sausages such as
   weisswurst, bratwurst, and/or
   knockwurst
1 tablespoon finely chopped
   fresh parsley leaves

In a large heavy skillet cook onion in butter over moderate heat, stirring occasionally, until golden. Add sauerkraut, broth or water, raisins, mustard, paprika, caraway seeds, and salt and pepper to taste and simmer, stirring occasionally, 10 minutes. Nestle sausages in sauerkraut and simmer, covered, 10 minutes, or until sausages are heated through.

Just before serving, sprinkle sauerkraut with parsley. Serves 2. May be doubled.

Caramel Pear Fool

1 15-ounce can pear halves, drained
¼ cup sugar
2 tablespoons water
½ teaspoon vanilla
½ cup well-chilled heavy cream

In a blender purée pears until smooth. Prepare a large bowl of ice and cold water.

In a dry small saucepan heat sugar over moderately high heat, without stirring, until it begins to melt, and continue cooking, swirling pan, until it is a golden caramel. Stir in water, pear purée, and vanilla carefully (mixture bubbles up) and cook, stirring, until caramel is dissolved. Remove pan from heat and set in large bowl of ice and cold water, stirring occasionally, until chilled.

In a chilled bowl beat cream until it holds stiff peaks and gently fold into caramel mixture until just combined and streaks are still visible.

Spoon fool into 2 stemmed glasses and chill until ready to serve. Serves 2. May be doubled.

Maharajah's Supper

**CHICKEN CURRY WITH
CHICK-PEAS AND BROCCOLI**

BASMATI RICE

FRIED PAPPADAMS
(STORE-BOUGHT)

SPICED POACHED PEARS

*Serves 2
(All recipes may be
doubled to serve 4)*

RICCARDO FALCHINI
VERNACCIA DI
SAN GIMIGNANO
1994

Maharajah's Supper

For visiting royalty, friends, or family, curries are an easy and delicious option for dinner. Set out small bowls of prepared chutney (try mango or lime), golden raisins, toasted coconut, and/or toasted almonds for sprinkling on top. Long-grain basmati rice, either steamed or prepared as a pilaf, is a perfect accompaniment. Prepare the rice before the other dishes as it will take the most time to cook. Pappadams, crisp wafer-thin lentil-flour breads, are available at Indian markets and in the international section of some supermarkets. They are also available by mail order from Adriana's Caravan, tel. (800) 316-0820. Follow the package instructions for shallow-frying or microwaving.

QUICK TIP:
- If you're rushed, pick up already-trimmed broccoli flowerets at the salad bar of your supermarket.

CHICKEN CURRY WITH CHICK-PEAS AND BROCCOLI

½ cup chopped onion
1 large garlic clove, minced
2 tablespoons vegetable oil
2 teaspoons curry powder
½ teaspoon ground cumin seeds
¼ teaspoon ground coriander seeds
⅛ teaspoon cinnamon
⅛ teaspoon cayenne, or to taste
1 fresh hot green chili, or to taste, seeded and minced (wear rubber gloves)
1 14- to 16-ounce can whole tomatoes, drained and chopped
1 skinless boneless whole chicken breast, cut into 1½-inch pieces
½ cup rinsed drained canned chick-peas
1 cup 1-inch broccoli flowerets

Accompaniment: cooked basmati rice

In a large heavy skillet cook onion and garlic in oil over moderate heat, stirring occasionally, until golden. Add curry powder, cumin, coriander, cinnamon, cayenne, chili, and tomatoes and simmer, stirring, 5 minutes. Add chicken and chick-peas and cook, covered, stirring occasionally, 10 minutes. Stir in broccoli and cook 10 minutes, or until broccoli is crisp-tender. Season chicken curry with salt.

Serve curry over rice. Serves 2. May be doubled.

SPICED POACHED PEARS

2 small firm-ripe Bosc or Bartlett
  pears (about 6 ounces each)
2 cups cranberry-raspberry
  juice cocktail
½ cup sugar
2 bay leaves
2 whole cloves
1 teaspoon julienne strips of
  orange zest

Core pears from bottom with a melon-ball cutter and peel, leaving stems intact.

In a 2-quart saucepan simmer pears in juice with remaining ingredients, uncovered, turning occasionally, until pears are tender but still hold their shape, about 10 minutes. Transfer pears to a plate with a slotted spoon, reserving poaching liquid, and chill, covered, in freezer 15 minutes.

While pears are chilling, boil reserved poaching liquid until reduced to about 1 cup. Pour sauce into a metal bowl set in a larger bowl of ice and cold water. Stir sauce until slightly cooled.

Serve pears in shallow bowls with some sauce and garnished with bay leaves. (Do not eat bay leaves.) Serves 2. May be doubled.

Photo on page 48

Leaner and Lighter Menus

Here are 10 low-fat menus using many of the leaner/lighter dishes that appear in the following chapters. Choose a menu whenever you want to enjoy a lighter meal; or mix and match menus for a whole day's worth of healthier eating. Any combination of our menus will be under the recommended daily totals of 2,000 calories and 30% of calories from fat, leaving you plenty of room to add snacks of fresh fruits and vegetables. To calculate the percentage of calories from fat multiply fat grams by 9 (because there are 9 calories per gram of fat) and divide by the total number of calories:

$$\frac{\text{fat grams} \times 9}{\text{total calories}} = \text{\% of calories from fat}$$

Breakfasts

BANANA GINGER WAFFLES (PAGE 128)
Per serving: 391 calories; 8 grams fat

FRESH ORANGE JUICE
Per serving: 83 calories; 1 gram fat

Each menu serving about: 474 calories; 9 grams fat (17% of calories from fat)

CURRIED POTATO AND EGG HASH (PAGE 127)
Per serving: 235 calories; 6 grams fat

WHOLE WHEAT TOAST WITH JAM
Per serving (1 slice): 125 calories; 2 grams fat

Each menu serving about: 360 calories; 8 grams fat (20% of calories from fat)

Brunch

CHILLED CANTALOUPE MINT SOUP (PAGE 75)
Per serving: 92 calories; 0 grams fat

GORGONZOLA AND SCALLION SOUFFLÉ (PAGE 133)
Per serving: 121 calories; 3 grams fat

Each menu serving about: 213 calories; 3 grams fat (13% of calories from fat)

Lunches

TURKEY PASTRAMI REUBENS (PAGE 123)
Per serving: 248 calories; 7 grams fat

CHILI POTATO CHIPS (PAGE 64)
Per serving: 140 calories; 1 gram fat

Each menu serving about: 388 calories; 8 grams fat (19% of calories from fat)

CHICKEN SPINACH NOODLE SOUP (PAGE 70)
Per serving: 382 calories; 7 grams fat

WATERCRESS, APPLE, AND DATE SALAD (PAGE 168)
Per serving: 225 calories; 3 grams fat

Each menu serving about: 607 calories; 10 grams fat (15% of calories from fat)

CITRUS GAZPACHO (PAGE 73)
Per serving: 97 calories; 1 gram fat

GRANDÉ CHICKEN AND BLACK BEAN BURRITOS (PAGE 119)
Per serving: 492 calories; 11 grams fat

Each menu serving about: 589 calories; 12 grams fat (18% of calories from fat)

ZUCCHINI STUFFED WITH CORN, BELL PEPPER, AND VEAL (PAGE 111)
Per serving: 252 calories; 8 grams fat

RICE SALAD WITH WATERCRESS (PAGE 146)
Per serving: 214 calories; 5 grams fat

Each menu serving about: 466 calories; 13 grams fat (25% of calories from fat)

Dinners

SAUTÉED CHICKEN WITH PEAR AND CIDER SAUCE (PAGE 121)
Per serving: 243 calories; 4 grams fat

STEAMED ACORN SQUASH WITH MOLASSES (PAGE 152)
Per serving: 151 calories; 0 grams fat

BLUEBERRY AND RASPBERRY COMPOTE WITH BASIL MINT SYRUP (PAGE 130)
Per serving: 131 calories; 1 gram fat

Each menu serving about: 525 calories; 5 grams fat (9% of calories from fat)

OVEN-ROASTED COD AND VEGETABLES (PAGE 79)
Per serving: 225 calories; 4 grams fat

RED POTATO SALAD WITH LEMON SCALLION DRESSING (PAGE 169)
Per serving: 203 calories; 1 gram fat

POACHED SPICED APPLE WITH LEMON YOGURT SAUCE (PAGE 177)
Per serving: 176 calories; 1 gram fat

Each menu serving about: 604 calories; 6 grams fat (9% of calories from fat)

GINGERED WHOLE RED SNAPPER WITH SHIITAKE MUSHROOMS (PAGE 83)
Per serving: 276 calories; 3 grams fat

ASIAN-STYLE NOODLES WITH CARROT AND SCALLION (PAGE 141)
Per serving: 172 calories; 3 grams fat

SESAME ASPARAGUS (PAGE 150)
Per serving: 81 calories; 3 grams fat

ALMOND COOKIE CRISPS (PAGE 176)
Per serving (3 cookies): 102 calories; 3 grams fat

Each menu serving about: 631 calories; 12 grams fat (17% of calories from fat)

ROASTED EGGPLANT CROSTINI (PAGE 65)
Per serving: 170 calories; 4 grams fat

RISOTTO WITH SWISS CHARD (PAGE 147)
Per serving: 291 calories; 5 grams fat

RASPBERRY MINT SORBET (PAGE 180)
Per serving: 249 calories; 1 gram fat

Each menu serving about: 710 calories; 10 grams fat (13% of calories from fat)

PORK MEDALLIONS WITH APPLE AND ONION (PAGE 102)
Per serving: 300 calories; 11 grams fat

STEAMED CAULIFLOWER WITH CARAWAY BUTTERMILK SAUCE (PAGE 151)
Per serving: 88 calories; 2 grams fat

ANGEL FOOD CAKE ORANGE TRIFLES (PAGE 172)
Per serving: 225 calories; 3 grams fat

Each menu serving about: 613 calories; 16 grams fat (23% of calories from fat)

THE RECIPES

First Courses

NOODLES AND SMOKED SALMON WITH DILL SAUCE

¼ pound fresh egg noodles
    or 3 ounces dried
¼ cup dry white wine
1½ tablespoons minced shallot
½ cup heavy cream
1 tablespoon chopped fresh dill
2 ounces thinly sliced smoked
    salmon, cut along grain
    into 2- by ¼-inch strips

Bring a kettle of salted water to a boil for noodles.

In a saucepan bring wine with shallot to a boil. Simmer wine until reduced to about 1 tablespoon and stir in cream. Bring mixture to a boil and simmer 5 minutes. Keep sauce warm, covered.

Cook noodles in boiling water, stirring occasionally, until *al dente*, about 3 minutes for fresh noodles or 6 minutes for dried. Drain noodles well in a colander and transfer to a heated large bowl.

Bring sauce just to a boil. Remove pan from heat and stir in dill. Pour sauce over noodles and toss well. Stir in salmon gently with a large fork and season pasta with salt and pepper. Serves 2. May be doubled.

Photo opposite

STEAMED SHRIMP WITH TARRAGON TOMATO CONCASSÉ

½ pound large shrimp (about 8),
    shelled, leaving tail and first shell
    section intact, and deveined
3 plum tomatoes, peeled, seeded,
    and cut into ¼-inch dice
2 teaspoons minced fresh tarragon
    leaves, or to taste
1 teaspoon extra-virgin olive oil
1 teaspoon white-wine vinegar

Garnish: fresh tarragon leaves

Season shrimp with salt and on a steamer rack set in a saucepan of boiling water steam shrimp, covered, until just cooked through, about 3 minutes. Transfer shrimp to a bowl and chill, covered, until cold, about 30 minutes.

While shrimp are chilling, in a small bowl stir together remaining ingredients and salt and pepper to taste. Toss shrimp in tomato *concassé* to season.

Arrange shrimp in a circle on 2 plates and mound tomato *concassé* in center of each plate. Garnish each serving with tarragon leaves. Serves 2. May be doubled.

Each serving: 136 calories, 3 grams fat (20% of calories from fat)

ARTICHOKES WITH HERBED ROASTED PEPPER VINAIGRETTE

2 artichokes
1 lemon half
2 teaspoons vegetable oil

For vinaigrette
⅓ cup chopped drained bottled roasted red pepper
¼ cup vegetable oil
1 tablespoon fresh lemon juice
1 tablespoon chopped fresh basil
½ teaspoon dried oregano, crumbled
¼ teaspoon minced garlic

Prepare artichokes:

Cut off stems of artichokes with a stainless-steel knife and discard. Break off tough outer leaves and cut off top fourth of artichokes. Snip off tips of artichoke leaves with kitchen scissors and rub cut edges with lemon half.

In a large saucepan arrange trimmed artichokes right sides up and add enough water to reach about 2 inches up side of pan. Drizzle artichokes with oil. Bring water to a boil, covered, and simmer artichokes until tender (test a leaf for doneness), 25 to 35 minutes.

Make vinaigrette while artichokes simmer:

In a blender blend together vinaigrette ingredients and salt and pepper to taste until emulsified.

Transfer artichokes with tongs to a colander to drain. Put each artichoke on a plate. Spoon some vinaigrette over each artichoke and serve remaining vinaigrette on the side. Serves 2. May be doubled.

YELLOW TOMATO SALAD WITH LEMONGRASS

Fresh lemongrass imparts a citrusy accent to our tomato salad. Peel off tough outer leaves until you find the pale tender inner part. Lemongrass is available at Asian markets or by mail order from Uwajimaya, tel. (800) 889-1928; yellow, pear, and currant tomatoes are available at specialty produce markets.

3 stalks fresh lemongrass, outer leaves discarded and ends trimmed
2 tablespoons vegetable oil
1 shallot, minced
2 teaspoons fresh lemon juice, or to taste
¼ teaspoon minced garlic
⅛ teaspoon finely grated fresh lemon zest
⅛ teaspoon ground coriander seeds cayenne to taste
2 medium yellow tomatoes (about 1 pound), sliced crosswise

Garnish: pear tomatoes, currant tomatoes, and/or cherry tomatoes

Thinly slice lower 5 inches of lemongrass stalks, reserving remainder for another use, and mince. In a small bowl whisk together lemongrass, oil, shallot, lemon juice, garlic, zest, coriander, cayenne, and salt to taste. Divide tomato slices between 2 plates and spoon dressing over them. Let salads stand at room temperature 30 minutes.

Garnish salads with small tomatoes. Serves 2. May be doubled.

Photo opposite

Yellow Tomato Salad with Lemongrass

Sausage and Pepper Stuffed Mushrooms

¼ pound Italian sausage
  (sweet or hot),
  casing discarded
¼ cup chopped red bell pepper
2 tablespoons chopped onion
2 tablespoons freshly grated
  Parmesan
2 teaspoons balsamic vinegar
8 large mushrooms (about
  ½ pound), stems discarded

Garnish: minced fresh parsley leaves

Preheat oven to 400° F. and lightly grease a small baking dish.

In a heavy skillet cook sausage, bell pepper, and onion over moderate heat, stirring and breaking up sausage, until sausage is cooked through. Drain mixture in a sieve and transfer to a bowl. Stir in Parmesan, vinegar, and salt and pepper to taste and divide sausage filling among mushroom caps, mounding it. Arrange mushrooms in baking dish and bake 12 minutes, or until tops are browned.

Sprinkle mushrooms with parsley. Serves 2. May be doubled.

Goat Cheese and Sun-Dried Tomato Quesadillas

4 ounces soft mild goat cheese,
  such as Montrachet, at room
  temperature
2 tablespoons cream cheese, softened
2 tablespoons coarsely chopped
  drained sun-dried tomatoes
  packed in oil
1½ tablespoons chopped fresh
  coriander sprigs
4 7- to 8-inch flour tortillas
2 tablespoons unsalted butter,
  melted

Accompaniment: tomato salsa

Preheat broiler.

In a bowl stir together cheeses, sun-dried tomatoes, coriander, and pepper to taste.

On a large baking sheet arrange 2 tortillas side by side and brush lightly with some butter. Turn tortillas over and divide cheese mixture between them, spreading evenly. Top cheese mixture with remaining tortillas. Brush tops lightly with some remaining butter and broil *quesadillas* about 4 inches from heat 1 to 2 minutes, or until tops are golden and crisp. Turn *quesadillas* carefully with a spatula and brush tops lightly with remaining melted butter. Broil *quesadillas* 1 minute more, or until tops are golden and crisp.

Cut *quesadillas* into wedges and serve with salsa. Serves 2. May be doubled.

Hors d'Oeuvres

FETA AND OLIVE PITA NACHOS

1 5- to 6-inch pita loaf
3 ounces feta cheese, crumbled
   or grated (about ½ cup)
⅓ cup Kalamata or other
   brine-cured black olives, pitted
   and chopped coarse
1 teaspoon sesame seeds

Preheat oven to 350° F.

Halve pita horizontally and quarter each round. In a shallow baking pan arrange pita triangles, rough sides up, and sprinkle with feta and olives. Sprinkle nachos with sesame seeds and pepper to taste and bake in middle of oven 10 minutes, or until golden. Makes 8 nachos, serving 2. May be doubled.

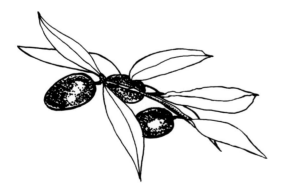

ZUCCHINI WHITE BEAN DIP

1 small zucchini, cut into
   ½-inch-thick rounds
1 small garlic clove, sliced
1 19-ounce can cannellini beans,
   rinsed and drained
¼ cup loosely packed fresh parsley
   leaves
1 tablespoon fresh lemon juice
⅛ teaspoon ground cumin

Accompaniments: crudités, such as carrot, celery, and red bell pepper, and/or pita toasts

On a steamer rack set in a small saucepan of boiling water steam zucchini and garlic, covered, 10 minutes, or until zucchini is soft. In a food processor purée zucchini and garlic with remaining ingredients and salt and pepper to taste.

Serve dip with crudités and/or pita toasts. Makes about 1½ cups, serving 2 generously. May be doubled.

Each serving without accompaniments:
202 calories, 1 gram fat
(4% of calories from fat)

Radishes with Chive Butter

In a small bowl with a fork stir together well butter, cream cheese, chives, zest, Tabasco, and salt to taste and transfer to a pastry bag fitted with a medium-sized open-star tip. Arrange radishes, cut sides up, on a platter. Put a parsley leaf on each radish half and pipe chive butter onto it. Chill radishes, covered loosely, until ready to serve. Makes 18 hors d'oeuvres, serving 2 generously. May be doubled.

Photo on left

RADISHES WITH CHIVE BUTTER

Piping simple fillings looks very impressive and can be done in a flash. If you don't have a pastry bag, simply snip off a small corner of a heavy-duty sealable plastic bag.

> 3 tablespoons unsalted butter, softened
> 1 tablespoon cream cheese, softened
> 1½ teaspoons minced fresh chives
> ⅛ teaspoon freshly grated lemon zest
> Tabasco to taste
> 9 radishes, leaves trimmed, leaving 1-inch stem, and radishes halved lengthwise
> 18 fresh flat-leafed parsley leaves

MELON, PROSCIUTTO, AND MINT KEBABS

> 6 3-inch wooden skewers
> 3 slices prosciutto or hot cappicola, halved lengthwise
> 12 fresh mint leaves
> 6 1-inch pieces cantaloupe
> 6 1-inch pieces honeydew melon
> 2 teaspoons balsamic vinegar

Onto a skewer thread end of a prosciutto or cappicola slice, 1 mint leaf, 1 piece cantaloupe, 1 piece honeydew, and another mint leaf. Weave prosciutto or cappicola slice around threaded ingredients and secure other end of slice on skewer. Assemble remaining kebabs in same manner with remaining prosciutto or cappicola, mint, and melons. On a large plate sprinkle kebabs with vinegar and chill, covered, until ready to serve. Makes 6 kebabs, serving 2. May be doubled.

CURRIED CHICKEN SATÉS WITH COCONUT PEANUT DIPPING SAUCE

1 tablespoon vegetable oil
1 tablespoon fresh lime juice
1 teaspoon curry powder
1 whole skinless boneless chicken breast, cut lengthwise into ¼-inch-thick slices
8 to 10 7-inch wooden skewers, soaked in water to cover 15 minutes

For dipping sauce
2 tablespoons sweetened flaked coconut
2 tablespoons smooth or chunky peanut butter
1 small garlic clove, chopped
1 tablespoon fresh lime juice
1 tablespoon soy sauce
3 tablespoons chopped fresh coriander sprigs
¼ teaspoon Asian chili oil or Tabasco, or to taste
2 tablespoons water

Prepare grill.

In a bowl stir together vegetable oil, lime juice, curry powder, and salt and pepper to taste and add chicken, tossing to coat. Onto skewers thread chicken slices lengthwise and on a large plate chill, covered, while making sauce.

Make dipping sauce:

In a blender blend together sauce ingredients and salt and pepper to taste until smooth and transfer to a bowl.

Grill *satés* on an oiled rack set 5 to 6 inches over glowing coals until cooked through, about 1½ minutes on each side. (Alternatively, *satés* may be grilled in batches in a hot well-seasoned ridged grill pan in same manner.)

Serve *satés* with dipping sauce. Makes about 8 *satés*, serving 2. May be doubled.

CHILI POTATO CHIPS

For our spicy crisp chips, use a fine sieve to dust the chili powder mixture evenly over the potato slices.

- 2 teaspoons chili powder
- 1 teaspoon sugar
- ¾ teaspoon salt, or to taste
- 1 ½-pound russet (baking) potato, unpeeled

Preheat oven to 325° F. Line a large baking sheet with parchment paper and lightly grease paper.

In a small bowl stir together chili powder, sugar, and salt. In a food processor fitted with 2-millimeter slicing disk, or with a *mandoline* or other hand-held slicing device, cut potato crosswise into paper-thin slices. Arrange slices in one layer on parchment and sprinkle with chili powder mixture. Bake potato slices 30 minutes, or until crisp and golden brown, and transfer immediately to racks to cool. Serves 2.

Each serving: 140 calories, 1 gram fat (6% of calories from fat)

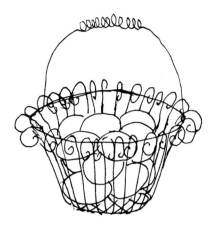

HERBED STUFFED EGGS

For an even fluffier egg filling for our stuffed eggs, press the yolks through a small sieve with a wooden spoon instead of mashing them with a fork.

- 4 hard-cooked large eggs
- 2 tablespoons mayonnaise
- 2 teaspoons fresh lemon juice
- 2 tablespoons finely chopped celery
- 3 tablespoons minced fresh herbs such as parsley, tarragon, dill, oregano, and/or chives

Halve eggs lengthwise and remove yolks. In a bowl mash yolks with a fork. Add remaining ingredients and salt and pepper to taste and combine well. Fill whites with yolk mixture, mounding it, and chill, covered, until ready to serve. Makes 8 stuffed eggs, serving 2. May be doubled.

ROASTED EGGPLANT CROSTINI

Select heavy eggplants that have shiny, taut skin and flesh that is neither too taut nor too firm. When pressed with a finger the vegetable should yield to slight pressure, but an indentation should not form.

$\frac{1}{2}$ pound eggplant, cut into $\frac{1}{4}$-inch dice

1 small yellow bell pepper, cut into $\frac{1}{4}$-inch dice

$\frac{1}{2}$ medium onion, cut into $\frac{1}{4}$-inch dice

1 small tomato, seeded and cut into $\frac{1}{4}$-inch dice

2 tablespoons minced fresh basil leaves

2 teaspoons balsamic vinegar

1 teaspoon olive oil

8 $\frac{1}{4}$-inch-thick slices French bread (about 2 inches in diameter), lightly toasted

Preheat oven to 450° F. and lightly grease a shallow baking pan.

In baking pan arrange eggplant, bell pepper, and onion in one layer and roast 20 minutes, or until tender. Transfer vegetables to a bowl and stir in tomato, basil, vinegar, oil, and salt and pepper to taste. Mound warm vegetable mixture on toasts. Makes 8 *crostini*, serving 2. May be doubled.

Each serving: 170 calories, 4 grams fat (21% of calories from fat)

MAPLE WALNUT CHEDDAR SPREAD

$\frac{1}{4}$ pound sharp Cheddar, grated

2 tablespoons unsalted butter, softened

2 tablespoons pure maple syrup

1 teaspoon paprika

$\frac{1}{4}$ cup lightly toasted walnuts, chopped

Accompaniment: water crackers or other unsalted crackers

In a food processor purée Cheddar, butter, syrup, paprika, and pepper to taste until smooth. Stir in walnuts and blend well. Transfer spread to a crock or bowl. Chill spread, covered, at least 30 minutes and up to 1 week.

Serve spread with crackers. Makes about 1 cup, serving 2 with leftovers. May be doubled.

Hot Soups

NEW ENGLAND CLAM CHOWDER

If time is tight, buy clams already shucked and chopped from your fishmonger. (You'll need about 1 pint to equal 25 medium hard-shelled clams.)

- 3 ounces salt pork, rind discarded and pork cut crosswise into ¼-inch strips
- 1 onion, chopped
- 2 small red potatoes, cut into ½-inch cubes
- 1 cup water
- 25 shucked medium hard-shelled clams, reserving ¾ cup liquor, chopped, or a 6½-ounce can minced clams, drained, and ¾ cup bottled clam juice
- 1½ cups half-and-half

Rinse salt pork and pat dry. In a heavy saucepan sauté salt pork over moderately high heat, stirring, until golden and transfer with a slotted spoon to paper towels to drain. Pour off all but 1½ tablespoons drippings. In drippings remaining in pan cook onion over moderately low heat, stirring, until softened and stir in potatoes and water. Simmer mixture, covered, 10 minutes, or until potatoes are just tender, and boil, uncovered, 12 minutes, or until most of liquid is evaporated. Stir in shucked clams and reserved liquor, or canned clams and bottled clam juice, and simmer 2 minutes. In a saucepan bring half-and-half just to a boil and stir into chowder with salt pork. Season chowder with salt and pepper. Makes about 4 cups, serving 2. May be doubled.

Photo opposite

CORNED BEEF, CABBAGE, AND LENTIL SOUP

- 1 onion, chopped
- 1 garlic clove, minced
- 1 tablespoon vegetable oil
- ½ cup lentils, picked over
- 2½ cups water
- 1½ cups beef broth
- 1 5-ounce piece cooked corned beef, cut into ¼-inch dice
- 2 cups chopped cabbage

In a 3-quart heavy saucepan cook onion and garlic in oil over moderately low heat, stirring, until softened. Add lentils, water, broth, and corned beef and simmer, covered, 30 minutes. Stir in cabbage and simmer, uncovered, until cabbage is tender, 5 to 7 minutes. Season soup with salt and pepper. Makes about 5½ cups, serving 2 generously. May be doubled.

New England Clam Chowder

CREAM OF ASPARAGUS SOUP

To trim asparagus, simply snap off the woody ends. This will remove any tough fibers.

   1 small onion, chopped
   1 tablespoon unsalted butter
   1 pound asparagus, trimmed and cut into 1-inch pieces
1½ cups chicken broth
   2 teaspoons fresh lemon juice
   ½ teaspoon freshly grated lemon zest
   ¾ teaspoon fresh thyme leaves or ¼ teaspoon dried thyme, crumbled
   ½ cup half-and-half

In a heavy saucepan cook onion in butter over moderately low heat, stirring, until softened. Add asparagus, broth, lemon juice, zest, and thyme and simmer, covered, 10 minutes, or until asparagus is very tender. With a slotted spoon transfer ½ cup soup solids to a small bowl and purée remaining soup in a blender or food processor, returning puréed soup and solids to pan. Add half-and-half and salt and pepper to taste and cook over moderate heat, stirring, until just hot. Makes about 3 cups, serving 2. May be doubled.

WHITE BEAN, GERMAN SAUSAGE, AND SPINACH SOUP

   1 onion, chopped fine
   2 tablespoons vegetable oil
   ½ pound *bratwurst* or *knockwurst*, quartered lengthwise and cut crosswise into ¼-inch-thick slices
   1 19-ounce can white beans, drained and rinsed (about 1⅔ cups)

   3 cups chicken broth
   2 cups coarsely chopped washed fresh spinach or half a 10-ounce package thawed frozen spinach
   2 teaspoons distilled white vinegar, or to taste
   1 teaspoon paprika

In a heavy saucepan cook onion in oil over moderate heat, stirring, until onion begins to brown. Add sausage and cook, stirring, 2 minutes. In a blender purée 1 cup beans with 1 cup broth and add to sausage mixture with whole beans, remaining 2 cups broth, spinach, vinegar, paprika, and salt and pepper to taste. Simmer soup 10 minutes, stirring occasionally. Makes about 5½ cups, serving 2 generously. May be doubled.

BLACK BEAN AND RICE SOUP WITH GARLIC

   1 19-ounce can black beans, drained and rinsed (about 1⅔ cups)
   2 cups water
   ¼ cup finely chopped red onion
   3 garlic cloves, minced
   ½ teaspoon ground cumin seeds
   1 teaspoon vegetable oil
1½ cups chicken broth
   ¼ cup long-grain white rice
   2 tablespoons chopped scallion
   1 teaspoon medium-dry Sherry if desired

In a blender purée ½ cup beans with 1 cup water. In a heavy 3-quart saucepan cook red onion, garlic, and cumin in oil over moderately low heat, stirring, until onion is softened. Add puréed beans, whole beans, remaining cup water, broth, and rice and simmer, stirring occasionally, until rice is tender, about 15 minutes. Stir in scallion, Sherry, and salt and pepper to taste. Makes about 4 cups, serving 2 generously. May be doubled.

Each serving: 337 calories, 4 grams fat (11% of calories from fat)

ROASTED RED PEPPER AND CORN SOUP

In this soup raw potato puréed with roasted peppers and broth works as a quick thickener without added fat or cream. (For a leaner dish, forego the bacon topping.)

- 4 slices bacon, chopped coarse
- 1 12-ounce jar roasted red peppers, rinsed and drained (about 1½ cups)
- 1 large russet (baking) potato (about ½ pound), peeled and cut into ½-inch cubes
- 3 cups chicken broth
- ½ cup chopped celery
- 1 cup fresh or frozen corn
- 1 tablespoon chopped fresh basil leaves
- ⅛ teaspoon cayenne, or to taste

In a heavy saucepan cook bacon over moderate heat, stirring occasionally, until crisp and transfer with a slotted spoon to paper towels to drain. Pour off all but 1 tablespoon drippings. In a blender purée roasted peppers and ⅓ cup potato with 1 cup broth and add to pan with remaining potato, remaining 2 cups broth, celery, corn, basil, cayenne, and salt to taste. Simmer soup, partially covered, stirring frequently, 15 minutes, or until potato is tender.

Serve soup sprinkled with reserved bacon. Makes about 5 cups, serving 2 generously. May be doubled.

ONION AND MUSHROOM SOUP GRATINÉ

You can enjoy this warming soup even if you don't have flameproof bowls. Simply make cheese toasts separately and float them on top of the soup.

- 2 onions (about ¾ pound), halved lengthwise and sliced crosswise
- 2 tablespoons unsalted butter
- 10 ounces mushrooms, chopped
- 2 tablespoons Scotch
- 2 cups beef broth
- 1 tablespoon soy sauce
- 2 ½-inch-thick slices Italian bread, lightly toasted
- ⅔ cup coarsely grated Gruyère or Swiss cheese (about 2 ounces)

In a heavy saucepan cook onions in butter over moderate heat, stirring occasionally, 15 minutes. Add mushrooms and Scotch and cook over moderately high heat, stirring, until most of liquid is evaporated. Stir in broth, soy sauce, and salt and pepper to taste. Bring soup to a boil, stirring, and simmer 3 minutes.

Preheat broiler.

Divide soup between 2 flameproof soup bowls. Float toasts on top and sprinkle with cheese. Broil soups about 2 inches from heat until cheese is melted and bubbling, about 1 minute. Makes about 3½ cups, serving 2. May be doubled.

CHICKEN SPINACH NOODLE SOUP

To keep this soup low in fat we used very little oil to soften the onion and celery. Stir constantly to make sure the vegetables don't burn, and if they begin to stick, add a spoonful of broth or water to loosen.

½ cup chopped onion
½ cup chopped celery
1 teaspoon olive oil
2 cups chicken broth
1½ cups water
2 ounces spaghetti, broken into 3-inch pieces
1 teaspoon fresh thyme leaves or a large pinch dried thyme, crumbled
1 bay leaf
2 medium carrots, halved lengthwise and sliced thin crosswise
¾ pound skinless boneless chicken breast, cut into ½-inch pieces
1 cup packed fresh spinach or Swiss chard leaves, chopped
¼ cup thinly sliced scallion greens

In a heavy 3-quart saucepan cook onion and celery in oil over moderately low heat, stirring, until softened. Add broth, water, spaghetti, thyme, and bay leaf and simmer 10 minutes. Stir in carrots, chicken, and spinach or Swiss chard and simmer until pasta is tender, about 5 minutes. Discard bay leaf and stir in scallions and salt and pepper to taste. Makes about 4 cups, serving 2. May be doubled.

Each Serving: 382 calories, 7 grams fat (16% of calories from fat)

CURRIED CHICKEN AND RICE SOUP WITH TOMATO

If you'd like to use leftover cooked chicken in place of the chicken breast in this soup, simply substitute 1 cup of cooked chicken cut into ½-inch pieces and add it along with the tomato.

1 small onion, chopped fine
1 tablespoon vegetable oil
1 garlic clove, minced
1 teaspoon finely grated peeled fresh gingerroot
1½ teaspoons curry powder
½ teaspoon ground cumin seeds
¼ cup long-grain white rice
1¼ cups water
1¼ cups chicken broth
½ pound skinless boneless chicken (white or dark meat), cut into ½-inch pieces
1 tomato, chopped (about 1 cup)
3 tablespoons chopped fresh chives

In a large heavy saucepan cook onion in oil over moderate heat, stirring, until light golden. Add garlic and gingerroot and cook, stirring, 1 minute. Add curry powder and cumin and cook, stirring, 30 seconds. Add rice and water. Bring liquid to a boil and simmer, covered, 5 minutes. Add broth and chicken and simmer, covered, 10 minutes. Stir in tomato and simmer, stirring occasionally, 2 minutes. Stir in chives and salt and pepper to taste. Makes about 5 cups, serving 2 generously. May be doubled.

WINTER VEGETABLE SOUP

  ½ cup thinly sliced white part of
     scallion
1½ tablespoons olive oil
  2 cups chicken broth
  1 large carrot, sliced thin
  1 boiling potato, peeled and cut
     into ¼-inch pieces
  ¼ teaspoon dried thyme, crumbled
  1 cup small broccoli flowerets

*Accompaniment: Parmesan scallion pretzels
  (page 135)*

In a large heavy saucepan cook scallion in oil over moderately low heat, stirring, until softened and add broth, carrot, potato, and thyme. Bring mixture to a boil and simmer 5 minutes. Add broccoli and salt and pepper to taste and simmer 5 to 7 minutes, or until vegetables are tender.

Serve with Parmesan scallion pretzels. Makes 3 cups, serving 2. May be doubled.

Photo below

Cold Soups

CHILLED ZUCCHINI SOUP WITH SCALLION STICKS

2¼ cups chopped zucchini
   (about ¾ pound)
¼ cup thinly sliced scallions including
   greens plus 1 tablespoon
   minced scallion greens
1 tablespoon olive oil
1 cup chicken broth
¾ teaspoon finely chopped fresh
   rosemary leaves or ¼ teaspoon
   dried rosemary, crumbled
1 tablespoon unsalted butter
3 slices firm white sandwich bread,
   crusts removed
½ cup half-and-half
1½ teaspoons fresh lemon juice

*Garnish: julienne strips of lemon zest and
   thinly sliced scallion greens*

In a heavy saucepan cook zucchini and ¼ cup sliced scallions in oil over moderately low heat, stirring, 4 minutes. Add broth and rosemary. Bring mixture to a boil and simmer 8 minutes, or until zucchini is very tender.

Preheat broiler.

While zucchini mixture is simmering, in a saucepan melt butter with 1 tablespoon minced scallion greens and salt to taste over moderate heat, stirring occasionally. Brush scallion butter on bread and cut into ½-inch wide sticks. Toast sticks on a baking sheet under broiler about 4 inches from heat 1 minute, or until golden.

In a blender or food processor purée zucchini mixture with half-and-half, lemon juice, and salt and pepper to taste. Transfer soup to a metal bowl set in a larger bowl of ice and cold water and chill, stirring occasionally, until cold.

Ladle soup into 2 bowls and garnish with zest and sliced scallion greens. Serve soup with scallion sticks. Serves 2. May be doubled.

Photo opposite

CITRUS GAZPACHO

1 cup finely chopped peeled seedless
  cucumber
½ cup finely chopped red bell pepper
½ cup finely chopped red onion
1 garlic clove, minced and mashed to
  a paste with 1 teaspoon salt
1½ cups chilled tomato vegetable juice
  such as V-8 juice

¼ cup chilled fresh orange juice
2 tablespoons fresh lime juice
  Tabasco to taste

In a bowl stir together all ingredients and
chill, covered, until cold, about 30 minutes. Makes about 4 cups, serving 2. May
be doubled.

Each serving: 97 calories, 1 gram fat
(9% of calories from fat)

CHILLED AVOCADO SOUP WITH CHILI CORIANDER CREAM

Our avocado soup is at its best served ice cold. The fastest way to chill this soup is to put it in an ice water bath in the refrigerator.

- 1½ ripe avocados (preferably California)
- 1 tablespoon fresh lemon or lime juice, or to taste
- ¾ cup low-salt chicken broth
- ¾ cup buttermilk
- 1 cup ice water plus additional to thin soup
- ½ teaspoon ground cumin, or to taste Tabasco to taste

For chili coriander cream

- 2 tablespoons sour cream
- 2 tablespoons plain yogurt
- 1 garlic clove, chopped
- ½ fresh *jalapeño* chili, or to taste, seeded and chopped (wear rubber gloves)
- 1 cup packed fresh coriander sprigs, washed well and spun dry

Garnish: fresh coriander sprigs

Halve and pit avocados. Peel avocados and in a blender or food processor purée with lemon or lime juice, broth, buttermilk, 1 cup ice water, cumin, Tabasco, and salt and pepper to taste until smooth. Transfer soup to a metal bowl and thin with ¼ to ½ cup additional ice water to reach desired consistency. Set bowl in a larger bowl of ice and cold water and chill soup, covered, stirring soup occasionally, until very cold, about 30 minutes. (Soup will discolor if kept more than 4 hours.)

Make chili coriander cream while soup is chilling:

In a blender or small food processor blend chili coriander cream ingredients with salt and pepper to taste, scraping down sides occasionally, until very smooth.

Serve soup drizzled with chili coriander cream and garnished with coriander sprigs. Makes about 3½ cups, serving 2 generously. May be doubled.

Photo on page 10

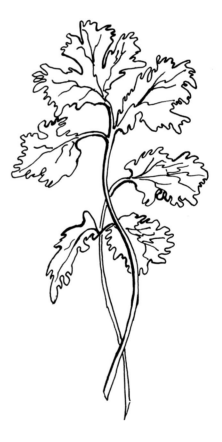

CHILLED YELLOW SQUASH BUTTERMILK SOUP WITH SHRIMP

Buttermilk, made from part-skim milk and cultures, is a rich-tasting low-fat alternative to cream or half-and-half in cold soups.

½ cup chopped onion
1 garlic clove, minced
½ teaspoon olive oil
8 large shrimp, shelled and deveined
2½ cups water
2 cups chopped yellow squash
1 cup buttermilk
2 teaspoons chopped fresh dill

In a heavy 3-quart saucepan cook onion and garlic in oil over moderately low heat, stirring, until softened. Add shrimp and water and simmer until shrimp are just cooked through, about 3 minutes. Transfer shrimp with a slotted spoon to a bowl.

Add squash to pan and simmer mixture until squash is very tender, about 10 minutes. While squash is simmering cut shrimp into ½-inch pieces and chill, covered.

In a blender purée squash mixture and transfer to a metal bowl set in a larger bowl of ice and cold water. Chill squash mixture, stirring occasionally, until cold, about 15 minutes. Stir in shrimp, buttermilk, dill, and salt and pepper to taste. Makes about 4 cups, serving 2. May be doubled.

Each serving: 159 calories, 3 grams fat (17% of calories from fat)

CHILLED CANTALOUPE MINT SOUP

To quickly remove rind from a whole melon, cut off thin slices from stem and blossom ends and set melon on a work surface with one cut side down. Slice off the rind from top to bottom, following the curve of the melon. Turn over the melon and carefully remove any remaining rind. Cut in half and scoop out seeds.

1 small cantaloupe, chilled
1 tablespoon fresh lime juice
1 tablespoon honey
1 cup cold water
2 teaspoons finely chopped fresh mint leaves

Halve cantaloupe and discard seeds and membranes. Scoop out 2 cups cantaloupe flesh, reserving remainder for another use. In a blender purée cantaloupe, lime juice, and honey and transfer to a bowl. Stir in water and mint and chill, stirring occasionally, until cold, about 30 minutes. Makes about 3 cups, serving 2. May be doubled.

Each serving: 92 calories, 0 grams fat (0% of calories from fat)

SALMON TERIYAKI WITH CARROTS AND ONIONS

Salmon ranges in color from pinkish-orange (with mild flavor) to deep red (with more pronounced flavor) depending on the variety and origin. If you prefer, ½-inch-thick fillets can be substituted for the steaks. The mirin, a sweet Japanese rice wine, can be found in Asian markets.

For teriyaki sauce
- ⅓ cup soy sauce
- 2½ tablespoons cider vinegar
- 2 tablespoons *mirin* (sweet Japanese rice wine) or medium-dry Sherry
- 2 tablespoons sugar
- 1½ tablespoons chopped peeled fresh gingerroot

- 2 ½-inch-thick salmon steaks
- 2 carrots, halved lengthwise and cut diagonally into ¼-inch-thick slices
- 1 onion, cut into ¼-inch-thick slices
- 1 tablespoon vegetable oil

Garnish: 2 scallion greens, cut decoratively

Make teriyaki sauce:

In a small saucepan simmer sauce ingredients, stirring, until sugar is dissolved and sauce is reduced to about ½ cup. Transfer sauce to a metal bowl set in a larger bowl of ice and cold water and cool to room temperature, stirring occasionally.

In a baking dish just large enough to hold salmon steaks in one layer marinate salmon in sauce, turning to coat, 15 minutes.

While salmon is marinating, in a large saucepan of boiling salted water blanch carrots and onion 2 minutes, or until crisp-tender, and drain in a colander. Transfer vegetables to a bowl of ice and cold water to stop cooking and drain well.

In a 10-inch heavy skillet (preferably cast iron) heat oil over moderately high heat until hot but not smoking. Transfer salmon to skillet with a slotted spatula, letting excess sauce drip into baking dish and reserving sauce. Reduce heat to moderate and cook salmon, turning once, until just cooked through and browned well, about 2½ minutes on each side. Transfer fish to 2 plates and pour off oil from skillet. Add vegetables to skillet and cook, stirring, 1 minute. Add reserved sauce and boil, stirring, 1 minute, or until thickened.

Spoon vegetables and sauce over salmon and garnish with scallion greens. Serves 2. May be doubled.

Photo opposite

PEPPERED CATFISH WITH ORANGE SALSA

If you're not sure whether you like catfish, try the farm-raised variety with its mild, clean taste. Here we've jazzed up our catfish with a spicy crust and zesty salsa.

For salsa
- 1 navel orange
- 1 tablespoon minced red onion
- 1 tablespoon fresh lime juice
- 2 teaspoons vegetable oil
- 2 teaspoons minced fresh mint leaves or minced fresh coriander sprigs
- ¼ teaspoon sugar

- 2 teaspoons paprika
- ¼ teaspoon cayenne, or to taste
- ½ teaspoon salt
- ¼ teaspoon freshly ground black pepper

- 2 catfish fillets (about 1 pound), rinsed and patted dry
- 1 tablespoon olive oil
- 1 tablespoon unsalted butter

Make salsa:

With a sharp knife cut peel and pith from orange and working over a small bowl cut orange sections free from membranes, letting sections drop into bowl. Stir in remaining salsa ingredients and let stand, covered, 30 minutes.

In a small bowl stir together paprika, cayenne, salt, and black pepper and sprinkle spice mixture on both sides of fillets, coating well. In a large skillet heat oil and butter over moderately high heat until foam subsides and sauté catfish 4 minutes on each side, or until just cooked through.

Transfer catfish fillets with a slotted spatula to 2 plates and serve with orange salsa. Serves 2. May be doubled.

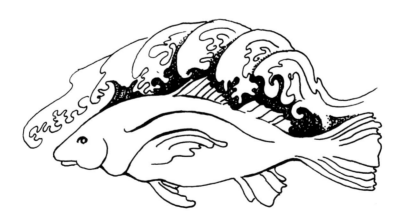

Oven-Roasted Cod and Vegetables

  2 plum tomatoes, quartered
  1 yellow bell pepper, cut into
      ½-inch-thick strips
  1 red onion, cut into
      ½-inch-thick wedges
  1 teaspoon vegetable oil
  ½ teaspoon fresh lemon juice
  3 teaspoons Worcestershire sauce
  2 6-ounce cod or scrod fillets
  1 teaspoon chopped fresh
      parsley leaves

Preheat oven to 500° F.

In a large shallow roasting pan toss tomatoes, bell pepper, and onion with oil and salt and pepper to taste and spread evenly in pan. Roast vegetables in middle of oven, stirring halfway through roasting, 15 minutes, or until edges begin to char.

In a bowl stir together lemon juice and 2 teaspoons Worcestershire and add fillets, turning to coat. Season fish with salt and pepper and add to roasting pan. Roast fish and vegetables until fish is just cooked through, about 6 minutes.

Transfer fish with a slotted spatula to 2 plates. Add parsley and remaining teaspoon Worcestershire to pan and stir vigorously to break up tomatoes slightly. Spoon vegetables over fish. Serves 2. May be doubled.

Each serving: 225 calories, 4 grams fat (16% of calories from fat)

Poached Cod with Parsley Almond Sauce

  2 ¾-inch-thick cod or scrod steaks
      (about 1 pound total)
  1 cup fresh parsley sprigs plus
      ½ cup leaves
  2 tablespoons whole blanched
      almonds
  2 tablespoons unsalted butter
  1 tablespoon fresh lemon juice
  1 tablespoon olive oil

In a deep heavy skillet just large enough to hold cod or scrod steaks in one layer spread parsley sprigs evenly and top with fish. Add enough cold water to just cover fish and season with salt. Bring water to a simmer and poach fish, covered, at a bare simmer 5 minutes, or until just cooked through. Transfer fish with a slotted spatula to 2 heated plates and reserve ¼ cup poaching liquid, discarding parsley sprigs and remaining liquid. Keep fish warm, covered loosely with foil.

In a small skillet cook almonds in butter over moderate heat, stirring, until golden. In a blender purée almonds, lemon juice, oil, and parsley leaves with reserved poaching liquid and salt and pepper to taste until smooth. Spoon sauce over fish. Serves 2. May be doubled.

NORWEGIAN-STYLE POACHED SALMON WITH ANCHOVY BUTTER

1½ tablespoons unsalted butter, softened
1½ tablespoons minced fresh parsley leaves
¾ teaspoon anchovy paste or mashed anchovy fillet
1 onion, sliced thin
4 cups water
⅓ cup distilled white vinegar
¼ cup sugar
½ teaspoon whole black peppercorns
1 teaspoon coriander seeds
½ teaspoon mustard seeds
1 teaspoon salt
2 1-inch-thick salmon steaks (each about ½ pound)

Accompaniment: rice with kale and tomatoes (recipe follows)

In a small bowl stir together butter, parsley, anchovy, and freshly ground black pepper to taste and cover anchovy butter.

In a saucepan bring all remaining ingredients except salmon steaks to a boil and simmer 15 minutes. Strain mixture through a fine sieve into a deep heavy skillet just large enough to hold salmon in one layer. Add salmon and bring liquid to a simmer. Poach salmon, covered, 8 minutes, or until just cooked through.

Divide rice between 2 plates. Transfer salmon with a slotted spatula to rice, letting poaching liquid drip into skillet, and top with anchovy butter. Serves 2. May be doubled.

Photo opposite

RICE WITH KALE AND TOMATOES

1 cup water
½ cup long-grain rice
1 small garlic clove, minced
1 tablespoon olive oil
1 14- to 16-ounce can whole tomatoes, drained, seeded, and chopped
2 cups finely chopped rinsed kale leaves

In a small heavy saucepan bring water to a boil and add rice and salt to taste. Cook rice, covered, over low heat 20 minutes, or until liquid is absorbed and rice is tender.

In a heavy skillet cook garlic in oil over moderately low heat, stirring, until golden. Add tomatoes and kale and cook, stirring occasionally, 3 minutes, or until kale is tender. Fluff rice with a fork and in a bowl combine well with kale mixture and salt and pepper to taste. Serves 2. May be doubled.

Photo opposite

Norwegian-Style Poached Salmon with Anchovy Butter; Rice with Kale and Tomatoes

FRIED FLOUNDER WITH SESAME SEED CRUST AND CUCUMBER SALAD

  1 small cucumber, peeled and
     sliced thin
  1 carrot, grated coarse
  2 tablespoons thinly sliced scallion
  1 tablespoon seasoned rice-wine
     vinegar
  1 tablespoon vegetable oil plus
     additional for frying
  2 6- to 8-ounce skinless flounder or
     orange roughy fillets
     cornstarch for dredging
  1 large egg
  ¼ teaspoon salt
  ⅔ cup fresh bread crumbs
  3 tablespoons sesame seeds

In a bowl toss together cucumber, carrot, scallion, vinegar, 1 tablespoon oil, and salt and pepper to taste and chill while preparing fish.

Pat fillets dry and season with salt and pepper. In 3 separate shallow dishes have ready cornstarch; egg beaten with salt; and bread crumbs combined with sesame seeds. Dredge each fillet in cornstarch to coat, shaking off excess, and dip in egg mixture, letting excess drip off. Dredge fillet in bread crumb mixture, pressing to make it adhere.

In a skillet just large enough to hold fillets in one layer heat ¼ inch of additional oil over moderately high heat until hot but not smoking and fry fish 1 minute on each side, or until golden brown. Transfer fish with a slotted spatula to paper towels to drain.

Serve fish with cucumber salad. Serves 2. May be doubled.

GRILLED MAHIMAHI WITH LIME, GARLIC, AND CUMIN

Mahimahi, also called dolphinfish (not the beloved mammal), is a warm-water fish caught off Hawaii, California, and Florida. When buying fillets, look for bright flesh of consistent color.

  ½ teaspoon finely grated lime zest
  2 tablespoons fresh lime juice
  3 tablespoons olive oil
  2 teaspoons honey
  1 garlic clove, minced
  ½ teaspoon ground cumin seeds
  ¼ teaspoon Tabasco
  2 ½-pound *mahimahi* (dolphinfish)
     fillets, rinsed and patted dry

Prepare grill.

In a shallow glass baking dish stir together zest, lime juice, oil, honey, garlic, cumin, Tabasco, and salt and pepper to taste. Add fillets, turning to coat, and marinate, covered and chilled, 20 minutes.

Transfer fillets to a plate and pour marinade into a small saucepan. Grill fish on an oiled rack set 5 to 6 inches over glowing coals 4 minutes on each side, or until just cooked through. Boil marinade 1 minute.

Transfer fish to 2 plates and spoon sauce over it. Serves 2. May be doubled.

GINGERED WHOLE RED SNAPPER WITH SHIITAKE MUSHROOMS

Red snapper is considered one of the best firm white-fleshed fish, and it is priced accordingly. The real thing has a large, heavy head; deep red-colored top; and is rosy pink near the belly. Have your fishmonger scale and gut the fish for you.

1   1½- to 2-pound whole red snapper, cleaned
¼   teaspoon dried hot red pepper flakes
1   tablespoon soy sauce
1   tablespoon medium-dry Sherry
4   ⅛-inch-thick slices peeled fresh gingerroot, cut into fine julienne strips (about 2 teaspoons)
1   carrot, cut into matchsticks
2   scallions, cut into matchsticks
5   medium *shiitake* mushrooms, stems discarded and caps cut into matchsticks

In a large deep skillet, fitted with a steamer rack and covered tightly, bring ½ inch of water to a boil.

Rinse snapper and pat dry with paper towels. Cut 5 slashes, about ½ inch deep, in snapper on each side and rub fish including slashes with red pepper flakes and salt to taste. Put fish on a heatproof plate about 1 inch smaller than skillet, trimming tail to fit if necessary. Drizzle fish on both sides with soy sauce and Sherry and top with remaining ingredients.

Arrange plate with fish on rack in skillet, covering skillet tightly, and steam fish over moderate heat 10 minutes, or until flesh closest to bone is opaque and fish is cooked through. Carefully remove plate from skillet and slide fish, vegetables, and juices onto a heated platter. Serves 2.

Each Serving: 276 calories, 3 grams fat (10% of calories from fat)

BAKED RED SNAPPER WITH DILLED MAYONNAISE

2   6-ounce red snapper fillets
¼   cup mayonnaise
2   teaspoons fresh lemon juice, or to taste
1   tablespoon minced fresh dill
½   teaspoon paprika

Preheat oven to 350° F. and butter a baking dish large enough to hold fillets.

In baking dish arrange fillets, skin sides down, in one layer. In a small bowl whisk together mayonnaise, lemon juice, dill, and pepper to taste and spread over snapper. Sprinkle fish with paprika and bake in middle of oven 10 minutes, or until just cooked through. Serves 2. May be doubled.

Sole with Citrus and Olive Sauce

2   6-ounce sole fillets
3   tablespoons fresh orange juice
3   tablespoons fresh lemon juice
2   tablespoons dry white wine
2   2-inch strips orange zest, cut into fine julienne strips
10 Kalamata or other brine-cured black olives, pitted and cut into slivers
½   teaspoon coarsely ground black pepper
1   teaspoon cornstarch dissolved in 1 tablespoon water
1   tablespoon cold unsalted butter, cut into bits
2   tablespoons finely chopped fresh parsley leaves

Preheat oven to 350° F.

In a baking dish just large enough to hold sole fillets in one layer stir together orange juice, lemon juice, wine, zest, olives, and pepper and add fish. Turn fish several times to coat well and marinate 5 minutes.

Bake fish in middle of oven 8 minutes, or until just cooked through. Transfer fish with a slotted spatula to 2 plates and keep warm, covered loosely with foil.

Transfer olive mixture in baking dish to a small saucepan. Stir cornstarch mixture and whisk into olive mixture. Bring sauce to a boil, whisking, until slightly thickened and remove pan from heat. Add butter, stirring until incorporated, and stir in parsley and salt to taste.

Spoon sauce over fish. Serves 2. May be doubled.

Photo opposite

Halibut Steak Veracruz

1   1-pound halibut steak, halved
1   medium onion, chopped
2   garlic cloves, chopped
¼   cup water
1   teaspoon vegetable oil
1   14- to 16-ounce can whole tomatoes including juice
¼   teaspoon sugar
⅛   teaspoon dried hot red pepper flakes, or to taste
¼   cup sliced pimiento-stuffed olives
2   teaspoons drained capers
1   teaspoon fresh lemon juice

Preheat oven to 450° F.

In a small baking dish arrange fish in one layer and season with salt. Chill fish, covered, while preparing sauce.

In a medium skillet bring onion, garlic, water, and oil to a boil, and simmer, covered, until onion is tender, about 10 minutes. Uncover skillet and cook mixture over moderate heat until liquid is evaporated and onion begins to brown. Add tomatoes with their juice, sugar, and red pepper flakes and simmer, stirring to break up tomatoes, 3 minutes, or until slightly thickened. Stir in olives, capers, and salt and pepper to taste and pour over fish.

Bake halibut in middle of oven 10 minutes, or until just cooked through. Sprinkle fish with lemon juice and serve with sauce. Serves 2. May be doubled.

Each Serving: 365 calories, 10 grams fat (25% of calories from fat)

Sole with Citrus and Olive Sauce; Lima Bean Purée with Olive Oil and Oregano (page 150)

BROILED CURRIED SWORDFISH STEAKS

When buying swordfish steaks look for gleaming bright white, gray, or pink-orange flesh with tight swirls. Ideally, find a fishmonger who will cut any fish into steaks or fillets from a whole fish.

2   1-inch-thick swordfish,
     mako shark, or tuna steaks
     (about ½ pound each)
3   tablespoons mayonnaise
1   tablespoon minced fresh coriander
     sprigs
2   teaspoons fresh lime juice
1   teaspoon curry powder

In a glass baking dish just large enough to hold fish steaks in one layer stir together mayonnaise, coriander, lime juice, curry powder, and salt and pepper to taste and add fish, rubbing mixture onto both sides. Chill fish, covered, 30 minutes.

Preheat broiler.

On foil-lined rack of a broiler pan broil fish about 6 inches from heat 5 minutes on each side, or until just cooked through. Serves 2. May be doubled.

GRILLED LEMON OREGANO SWORDFISH WITH CUCUMBER YOGURT SAUCE

2   6-ounce pieces swordfish
     (about 1 inch thick)
1   tablespoon fresh lemon juice
1   teaspoon dried oregano, crumbled
1   medium cucumber, peeled and
     seeded
⅓   cup low-fat yogurt
1   tablespoon chopped fresh mint
     leaves
½   teaspoon chopped garlic, mashed to
     a paste with ¼ teaspoon salt

Accompaniment: lemon wedges

Prepare grill.

In a shallow glass dish sprinkle both sides of fish with lemon juice, oregano, and salt and pepper to taste and marinate, covered and chilled, while preparing sauce.

Shred cucumber on large holes of a 4-sided grater. Wrap cucumber in a clean kitchen towel and squeeze to extract most of liquid. In a bowl stir together cucumber, yogurt, mint, garlic paste, and salt and pepper to taste.

Grill fish on a lightly oiled rack set 5 to 6 inches over glowing coals until just cooked through, about 4 minutes on each side.

Divide cucumber sauce between 2 plates and top with fish. Serve fish with lemon wedges. Serves 2. May be doubled.

Each Serving: 244 calories, 7 grams fat
(26% of calories from fat)

PROSCIUTTO-AND-BASIL-WRAPPED TUNA KEBABS

Tuna ranges from pale pink flesh (albacore) to deep red (bluefin and yellowfin) and is the most beeflike fish, making it ideal for grilling. When buying tuna steak look for even color; the blackish part of the flesh has a strong fishy taste, so have your fishmonger trim it off for you.

¼ cup olive oil
2 tablespoons fresh lemon juice
1 teaspoon Dijon mustard
1 1-inch-thick tuna steak
  (about 12 ounces), cut into
  2- by 1-inch pieces
10 whole large basil leaves
5 thin slices prosciutto
  (about ¼ pound),
  halved lengthwise

Prepare grill.

In a small bowl whisk together oil, lemon juice, mustard, and salt and pepper to taste. Wrap each piece of tuna with a basil leaf and then with prosciutto and thread pieces onto 4 metal skewers, leaving space between pieces. Brush kebabs with some dressing. Grill kebabs on a rack set 5 to 6 inches over glowing coals, turning kebabs and brushing with dressing, 7 to 10 minutes, or until tuna is just cooked through. Serves 2. May be doubled.

TOMATO AND BALSAMIC VINEGAR BAKED BLUEFISH

Bluefish is a full-flavored fish, best prepared with acidic ingredients to offset its oily richness—here we've used tomatoes and slightly sweet balsamic vinegar. Since bluefish becomes stronger in flavor as it ages, be sure to cook it the day you buy it.

2 6-ounce bluefish fillets
1 tomato, sliced thin
1 garlic clove, minced
⅓ cup balsamic vinegar
½ teaspoon dried oregano, crumbled

Preheat oven to 400° F.

Season bluefish with salt and pepper. In a baking dish just large enough to hold fillets in one layer arrange bluefish, skin sides down, and top with tomato slices, overlapping slightly, and garlic. Pour vinegar over top and sprinkle with oregano. Bake bluefish in middle of oven, basting occasionally with pan juices, 15 minutes, or until just cooked through. Serves 2. May be doubled.

CURRIED CHILI SHRIMP WITH SCALLION RICE

Canned unsweetened coconut milk is a quick, delicious alternative to making your own from grated fresh coconut. We particularly like the Chaokoh brand, which is widely available in Asian markets and many supermarkets.

2 teaspoons salt
⅔ cup long-grain white rice
For sauce
2 small shallots, minced
1 tablespoon minced peeled fresh gingerroot
1 garlic clove, minced
1½ teaspoons minced bottled pickled *jalapeño* (wear rubber gloves), or to taste
1 teaspoon salt
1 tablespoon vegetable oil
⅛ teaspoon turmeric
1 teaspoon curry powder
1 small onion, sliced thin crosswise
½ cup well-stirred unsweetened canned coconut milk
½ cup water

⅓ cup finely chopped white part of scallion plus ¼ cup thinly sliced scallion greens
1 tablespoon unsalted butter
¾ pound large shrimp (about 12), shelled, leaving tail and first shell section intact, and deveined

In a kettle bring 4 quarts water to a boil with salt. Sprinkle in rice, stirring until water returns to a boil, and boil 10 minutes. While rice is boiling, bring a large saucepan of water to a boil for steaming boiled rice.

In a large sieve drain rice and rinse. Set sieve over pan of boiling water and steam rice, covered with a kitchen towel and lid, 15 minutes, or until fluffy and dry.
Make sauce while rice is steaming:

On a work surface with flat side of a heavy knife or with a mortar and pestle mash together shallots, gingerroot, garlic, *jalapeño*, and salt until mixture forms a coarse paste. In a heavy skillet heat oil over moderate heat until hot but not smoking and cook paste, stirring, 1 minute. Add turmeric, curry powder, and onion and cook over moderately low heat, stirring, 2 minutes. Stir in coconut milk and water and simmer 4 minutes, or until sauce is reduced to about ½ cup.

In a skillet cook white part of scallion in butter over moderately low heat, stirring occasionally, until softened and in a bowl toss steamed rice with cooked scallion, scallion greens, and salt and pepper to taste.

Add shrimp in one layer to sauce and cook, turning once, 3 minutes, or until just cooked through. Toss scallion rice with about ¼ cup sauce.

Divide rice between 2 plates and top with shrimp and remaining sauce. Serves 2 generously. May be doubled.

Photo opposite

Curried Chili Shrimp with Scallion Rice

GLAZED BROILED SHRIMP AND SCALLIONS

Caramelized sugar acts as a sauce thickener and adds a slightly sweet, smoky essence. The darker you let the caramel become, the richer the flavor— but don't let it blacken or the sauce will taste acrid.

¾ pound large shrimp (about 12), shelled and deveined
6 scallions, cut into 1½-inch pieces
2 tablespoons soy sauce
2 tablespoons water
1 tablespoon fresh lemon juice
1 tablespoon distilled white vinegar
1½ tablespoons sugar
1 tablespoon chopped fresh rosemary leaves

Preheat broiler.

Season shrimp and scallions with salt and arrange in one layer on rack of broiler pan. Broil shrimp and scallions about 4 inches from heat 5 minutes, or until shrimp is just cooked through.

In a small bowl stir together soy sauce, water, lemon juice, and vinegar. In a dry small heavy skillet heat sugar over moderate heat, without stirring, until it begins to melt. Continue cooking sugar, swirling skillet, until it turns a golden caramel and remove skillet from heat. Carefully add soy sauce mixture (mixture will bubble) and simmer, stirring, until caramel is dissolved and sauce is reduced to a syrupy consistency. Add shrimp, scallions, and rosemary to sauce, tossing to coat. Serves 2. May be doubled.

Each Serving: 191 calories, 2 grams fat (9% of calories from fat)

GRILLED SHRIMP WITH OLIVES AND FETA

If you find that your feta is too salty, soak it in cold water in the refrigerator for 1 to 2 hours and pat dry. Once soaked, however, you should use the feta immediately.

¼ cup Kalamata or other brine-cured black olives, pitted and chopped
1 small vine-ripened tomato, chopped coarse
1½ teaspoons chopped fresh oregano leaves or ½ teaspoon dried oregano, crumbled
½ teaspoon minced garlic
¼ cup olive oil (preferably extra-virgin)
1 tablespoon red-wine vinegar
¾ pound large shrimp (about 12), shelled and deveined
¼ cup crumbled feta

Accompaniment: crusty peasant-style bread

In a bowl stir together olives, tomato, oregano, garlic, 3 tablespoons oil, vinegar, and pepper to taste.

In a small bowl toss shrimp with remaining tablespoon oil and salt and pepper to taste. Heat a well-seasoned ridged grill pan over high heat until hot and grill shrimp 2 to 3 minutes on each side, or until just cooked through.

In a shallow dish toss shrimp with olive mixture and let stand 15 minutes.

Sprinkle shrimp with feta and serve with bread. Serves 2. May be doubled.

SPICY SKILLET SHRIMP WITH SHERRY

½ cup chopped scallion
1 teaspoon minced garlic
1 teaspoon chili powder
¼ teaspoon salt
⅛ teaspoon cayenne
3 tablespoons unsalted butter
¾ pound medium shrimp (about 16), shelled and deveined
1 tablespoon medium-dry Sherry
2 teaspoons Worcestershire sauce
1 teaspoon fresh lemon juice
2 tablespoons minced fresh parsley leaves

Accompaniment: steamed rice

In a large skillet sauté scallion, garlic, chili powder, salt, and cayenne in butter over moderately high heat, stirring, 1 minute. Add shrimp and sauté, stirring, 2 minutes. Add Sherry, Worcestershire sauce, and lemon juice and simmer, stirring, 1 minute. Stir in parsley.

Serve shrimp with rice. Serves 2. May be doubled.

WHITE CLAM PIZZAS

Whole pita loaves make a quick substitute for pizza dough. With this low-fat creamy-tasting topping, you won't miss the cheese.

⅓ cup low-fat (1%) milk
2 teaspoons all-purpose flour
1 6½-ounce can minced clams, drained, reserving 2 tablespoons juice
½ cup chopped seeded plum tomato (about 1 large)
1 tablespoon chopped fresh parsley leaves
1 teaspoon minced garlic
½ teaspoon dried oregano, crumbled
2 6- to 7-inch pita loaves

Preheat oven to 425° F.

In a small heavy saucepan whisk together milk, flour, and reserved clam juice and simmer, whisking, until slightly thickened, about 2 minutes.

In a small bowl stir together clams, tomato, parsley, garlic, and oregano. On a baking sheet toast whole pita loaves in middle of oven 2 minutes on each side. Remove sheet from oven and spread sauce on pitas, leaving a ½-inch border around edge. Sprinkle pizzas with clam mixture and season with pepper. Bake pizzas 8 minutes, or until sauce begins to bubble. Serves 2. May be doubled.

Each serving: 249 calories, 2 grams fat (7% of calories from fat)

GRILLED CLAMS WITH TOMATO AND OLIVE SALSA

  1   cup chopped seeded vine-ripened
       tomato
  ¼   cup chopped pitted Kalamata or
       other brine-cured black olives
  2   tablespoons chopped scallion
  2   tablespoons chopped fresh
       basil leaves
  1   teaspoon minced garlic
  1⅓   tablespoons fresh lemon juice
  ¼   cup olive oil
 16   small (2-inch) hard-shelled clams,
       scrubbed

Preheat grill.

In a small bowl stir together all ingredients except clams and season with salt and pepper.

Grill clams on a rack set 5 to 6 inches over glowing coals, covered, 3 minutes. Turn clams over and grill, covered, transferring with tongs as they open to a small platter, 5 to 8 minutes. (Discard any unopened clams.)

Serve clams in shells with salsa. Serves 2 as a light entrée. May be doubled.

LINGUINE WITH WHITE CLAM SAUCE AND TOMATO

  ¼   pound dried *linguine*
  2   tablespoons minced shallot
  1   small garlic clove, minced
  ¼   cup finely chopped celery
  3   tablespoons unsalted butter
  ½   cup dry white wine
  1   cup water
 18   small (2-inch) hard-shelled clams,
       scrubbed
  1   tablespoon all-purpose flour
  ¼   cup minced fresh parsley leaves
  ¼   teaspoon dried thyme,
       crumbled
  1   8¼-ounce can whole tomatoes,
       drained, seeded, and chopped

Garnish: fresh parsley sprigs

Accompaniments: Parmesan; and onion and black pepper flatbread (page 134)

Bring a large saucepan of salted water to a boil for *linguine.*

In a skillet cook shallot, garlic, and celery in butter over moderately low heat, stirring occasionally, until vegetables are softened.

While vegetables are cooking, in another large saucepan bring wine and 1 cup water to a boil. Add clams and steam, covered, transferring with tongs as they open to a bowl, 5 to 10 minutes. (Discard any unopened clams.) Reserve 6 clams in their shells and 1 cup cooking liquid. Remove remaining 12 clams from shells and chop coarse.

Whisk flour into vegetables and cook over moderately low heat, whisking, 3 minutes. Whisk in reserved cooking liquid

Linguine with White Clam Sauce and Tomato; Onion and Black Pepper Flatbreads (page 134)

and bring to a boil. Stir in parsley, thyme, and salt and pepper to taste and simmer sauce, stirring occasionally, 5 minutes.

While sauce is cooking, cook *linguine* in boiling water until *al dente*, about 8 minutes and drain well in a colander.

Stir chopped clams and tomatoes into sauce and cook over moderate heat, stirring,

until clams are just heated through. Add *linguine* to clam sauce, tossing to combine.

Transfer *linguine* to a heated platter and arrange reserved clams around it. Garnish pasta with parsley sprigs and serve with Parmesan and onion and black pepper flatbread. Serves 2. May be doubled.

Photo above

LOBSTER SALAD RÉMOULADE

"Chicken" lobsters (lobsters that weigh just under 1 pound) and "culls" (lobsters with one claw missing) are good choices for this salad since they're a better value than large whole lobsters.

     2 1-pound live lobsters
    ½ cup chopped celery
    ¼ cup mayonnaise
     2 tablespoons minced scallion
     2 teaspoons fresh lemon juice, or
        to taste
     1 teaspoon Dijon mustard
     1 teaspoon drained bottled
        horseradish
     1 teaspoon paprika
    ¼ teaspoon Tabasco
     1 ripe avocado (preferably California)

Into a large kettle of boiling salted water plunge lobsters and boil, covered, 8 minutes from time water returns to a boil. Transfer lobsters with tongs to a colander and rinse under cold water until cool enough to handle. Break off claws at body and crack them. Remove claw meat and cut into ¾-inch pieces. Halve lobsters lengthwise along undersides. Remove meat from tails and cut into ¾-inch pieces. In a large bowl combine claw meat and tail meat. Break off legs at body and reserve for another use. Remove meat from body cavities near leg joints and add to bowl.

In a small bowl stir together all remaining ingredients except avocado and season with salt and pepper. Add *rémoulade* sauce to lobster and combine well.

Halve and pit avocado. Arrange each half on a plate and divide salad between them. Serves 2. May be doubled.

MUSSELS MARINARA WITH LINGUINE

Remove the "beard"—the tuft of filament a mussel uses to cling to rocks—by pulling it toward the smaller end of the shell and scrub shells well under cold running water.

     6 ounces dried *linguine*
     1 teaspoon vegetable oil
     1 medium onion, chopped
     1 large garlic clove, minced
     1 16-ounce can whole tomatoes
        including juice
     2 tablespoons dry vermouth
    ½ teaspoon ground coriander seeds
     1 pound mussels (preferably
        cultivated), scrubbed well in
        several changes of water and
        beards pulled off
     1 tablespoon chopped fresh
        parsley leaves

Bring a large saucepan of salted water to a boil for *linguine*.

In a non-stick skillet heat oil over moderately high heat until hot but not smoking and sauté onion, stirring occasionally, until translucent, about 5 minutes. Add garlic and sauté, stirring, 1 minute. Add tomatoes with juice, vermouth, coriander, and salt and pepper to taste, stirring to break up tomatoes, and simmer, stirring occasionally, until sauce is slightly thickened, about 10 minutes.

Cook *linguine* in boiling water until *al dente*, about 10 minutes, and drain in a colander. While pasta is cooking, add mussels to sauce and simmer, covered, 5 minutes, or until mussels are opened. (Discard any unopened mussels.)

In a heated large bowl toss *linguine* with sauce and mussels and sprinkle with parsley. Serves 2. May be doubled.

Each serving: 458 calories, 7 grams fat (14% of calories from fat)

CRAB CAKES WITH PIMIENTO AND CAPERS

½ pound lump crab meat, picked over
⅓ cup fresh bread crumbs
2 tablespoons drained chopped pimiento
2 tablespoons thinly sliced scallion
2 tablespoons mayonnaise
1 tablespoon drained capers
1½ teaspoons fresh lemon juice
1 egg white, beaten lightly
¼ teaspoon salt
1 tablespoon vegetable oil
1 tablespoon unsalted butter

Accompaniments: lemon wedges and tartar sauce

In a bowl stir together crab, bread crumbs, pimiento, scallion, mayonnaise, capers, lemon juice, egg white, salt, and black pepper to taste gently but thoroughly and form into 4 patties, each about ½ inch thick.

In a large heavy skillet heat oil and butter over moderately high heat until foam subsides and sauté patties, turning carefully, 4 minutes on each side, or until golden brown and crisp.

Serve crab cakes with lemon wedges and tartar sauce. Serves 2. May be doubled.

SAUTÉED SOFT-SHELLED CRABS WITH LEMON AND FRESH CORIANDER

4 soft-shelled crabs (about ¾ pound), cleaned by fishmonger
¾ cup milk
all-purpose flour seasoned with salt and pepper for dredging
1½ tablespoons vegetable oil
1½ tablespoons unsalted butter
¼ cup fresh lemon juice
1½ tablespoons finely chopped fresh coriander sprigs

In a bowl let crabs soak in milk 15 minutes. Remove crabs from milk, letting excess drip off, and dredge in flour, coating well. In a large skillet heat oil and butter over moderately high heat until foam subsides and sauté crabs 4 minutes on each side, or until golden brown. Divide crabs between 2 plates. Pour off fat from skillet. Add lemon juice and boil, scraping up brown bits, about 1 minute.

Spoon sauce over crabs and sprinkle with coriander. Serves 2. May be doubled.

Sautéed Scallops with Watercress and Corn Salad

1 tablespoon balsamic vinegar
¼ teaspoon Dijon mustard
3 tablespoons olive oil
½ pound sea scallops
2 tablespoons minced shallot
1 large bunch watercress, coarse stems discarded and sprigs rinsed and spun dry (about 3 cups)
1 carrot, shredded
½ cup cooked fresh or thawed frozen corn

In a small bowl whisk together vinegar, mustard, 2 tablespoons oil, and salt and pepper to taste until combined well.

Pat scallops dry and season with salt and pepper. In a skillet (preferably non-stick) just large enough to hold scallops in one layer heat remaining tablespoon oil over moderately high heat until hot but not smoking and sauté scallops 2 minutes on each side, or until golden and just cooked through. With a slotted spoon transfer scallops to a bowl and keep warm. To skillet add shallot and about 1 tablespoon vinaigrette and cook over moderate heat, stirring, until shallot is softened. Remove skillet from heat. Add scallops and shake skillet to coat them with shallot mixture. In another bowl toss watercress, carrot, and corn with remaining vinaigrette.

Divide salad between 2 plates and arrange scallops around each salad. Serves 2 as a light entrée. May be doubled.

Photo opposite

Spicy Coconut Scallops with Duck Sauce

¾ pound sea scallops
¼ cup soy sauce
all-purpose flour seasoned with salt and pepper for dredging
2 eggs, beaten lightly
½ cup sweetened flaked coconut
⅓ cup dry bread crumbs
½ teaspoon dried hot red pepper flakes
vegetable oil for frying

Accompaniment: bottled Chinese duck sauce

In a small bowl stir together scallops and soy sauce and marinate, covered and chilled, 15 minutes.

In 3 separate shallow dishes have ready flour; egg; and coconut combined with bread crumbs and red pepper flakes. Drain scallops well and dredge in flour, shaking off excess. Dip each scallop in egg, letting excess drip off, and coat well with coconut mixture. In a large heavy skillet heat ½ inch oil over moderately high heat until hot but not smoking and fry scallops 1 minute on each side, or until golden, transferring to paper towels to drain.

Serve scallops with duck sauce. Serves 2. May be doubled.

FETTUCCINE WITH OYSTER FENNEL CREAM SAUCE

½ pound fettuccine
½ cup thinly sliced shallot
1 small fennel bulb (sometimes called anise), trimmed and sliced thin (about ½ pound)
3 tablespoons unsalted butter
¼ cup medium-dry Sherry
1 pint shucked oysters, drained, reserving oyster liquor, and chopped coarse
¾ cup heavy cream
2 teaspoons fresh lemon juice, or to taste
⅛ teaspoon fennel seeds, or to taste
¼ cup minced fresh parsley leaves

Bring a large saucepan of salted water to a boil for fettuccine.

In a large skillet cook shallot and fennel in butter, covered, over moderate heat, stirring occasionally, 12 minutes, or until fennel is just tender.

Cook pasta in boiling water until *al dente*, about 8 minutes, and drain in a colander.

While fettuccine is cooking, stir Sherry and reserved oyster liquor into fennel mixture and boil, uncovered, 2 minutes. Stir in cream, lemon juice, fennel seeds, oysters, and salt and pepper to taste and simmer, stirring, 3 minutes, or until edges of oysters curl. Remove skillet from heat.

Add fettuccine to oyster sauce with parsley and salt and pepper to taste and toss to combine well. Serves 2 generously. May be doubled.

GRILLED SQUID SALAD WITH LIME VINAIGRETTE

Vinaigrettes are usually made with oil, but here, the slight sweetness and low acidity of rice wine vinegar balances the smokiness of grilled squid without oil. You'll want to try our lime vinaigrette, the perfect dressing for a leaner/lighter dish, with other grilled fish and shellfish as well. And be sure to buy squid already cleaned by your fishmonger.

¾   pound cleaned squid
       (bodies and tentacles)
½   teaspoon freshly grated lime zest
1½ tablespoons fresh lime juice
1   tablespoon seasoned rice vinegar
¼   teaspoon dried hot red pepper
       flakes
1   small red onion, sliced very thin
2   cups shredded romaine
¼   cup loosely packed fresh
       coriander sprigs, washed well,
       spun dry, and chopped

Prepare grill.

Season squid with salt and pepper. Grill squid on a lightly-oiled rack set 4 to 5 inches over glowing coals, turning halfway through cooking, 6 minutes, or until cooked through. Remove squid to a cutting board and cool slightly. Cut squid bodies crosswise into ¼-inch-thick rings and quarter tentacles. (Alternatively, squid may be grilled in a heated well-seasoned grill pan in same manner.)

In a large bowl stir together zest, lime juice, vinegar, and red pepper flakes and add onion, squid, romaine, and coriander. Toss salad and season with salt and black pepper. Serves 2 as a light entrée. May be doubled.

Each serving: 191 calories, 3 grams fat (14% of calories from fat)

CURRIED PORK CHOPS WITH BRANDIED PEACH AND CRAB APPLE CHUTNEY

Pork can be a quick entrée when cooked in smaller cuts, such as our 1-inch chops. Here we pan-fry curry-rubbed chops, then briefly simmer them in a vinegared peach syrup that thickens to a delicious sauce. No one will ever know that you used bottled spiced crab apples and brandied peaches to make our "homemade" chutney. These condiments are available in many supermarkets.

 1 onion, diced
1½ tablespoons vegetable oil
 2 teaspoons balsamic vinegar
 1 teaspoon curry powder
 2 bottled brandied peaches
    (such as Raffetto's), drained,
    reserving ¼ cup syrup, and diced
 4 bottled whole spiced crab apples
    (such as Raffetto's), cored and diced
 1 teaspoon minced fresh
    parsley leaves
 2 1-inch-thick pork chops
 ½ teaspoon coarse salt
 ½ teaspoon freshly ground
    black pepper

In a small skillet cook onion in 1 tablespoon oil over moderately low heat, stirring, until softened and stir in 1 teaspoon vinegar and ¼ teaspoon curry powder. Transfer mixture to a small bowl and stir in peaches, crab apples, and parsley.

Pat pork chops dry. In a small bowl stir together remaining ¾ teaspoon curry powder, salt, and pepper and sprinkle on both sides of pork chops, rubbing it in. In a 9-inch heavy non-stick skillet heat remaining ½ tablespoon oil over moderately high heat until hot but not smoking and brown pork chops, about 3 minutes on each side. Pour off fat from skillet and reduce heat to moderately low. Add reserved peach syrup and remaining teaspoon vinegar and simmer, covered, 10 minutes, or until meat is just cooked through. Transfer pork chops to plates. Boil pan juices until thickened, about 15 seconds, and spoon over pork chops.

Serve pork chops with chutney. Serves 2. May be doubled.

Photo opposite

Curried Pork Chops with Brandied Peach and Crab Apple Chutney;
Brussels Sprouts and Onions with Dill (page 151)

PORK MEDALLIONS WITH APPLE AND ONION

- 6 ounces pork tenderloin, cut crosswise into ¼-inch thick slices
- 2 tablespoons all-purpose flour seasoned with salt and pepper
- ¾ cup chicken broth
- ½ cup apple juice
- 1½ tablespoons Dijon mustard
- 1 tablespoon vegetable oil
- 1 medium onion, sliced thin
- 1 Granny Smith apple, peeled and chopped

In a small bowl toss pork in seasoned flour to coat. In a bowl whisk together broth, juice, and mustard.

In a non-stick skillet heat oil over moderately high heat until hot but not smoking and brown pork on both sides, transferring to a plate. Add onion and apple to skillet and cook over moderate heat until golden and just tender, about 5 minutes. Stir in broth mixture and simmer until liquid is slightly thickened. Return pork to skillet and cook just until hot, about 1 minute. Serves 2. May be doubled.

Each serving: 300 calories, 11 grams fat (33% of calories from fat)

JAMAICAN-SPICED PORK TENDERLOIN

Simple and succulent, this pork tenderloin is first grilled for rich smoky flavor, then quickly roasted in a hot oven to finish cooking. Our Jamaican spice paste adds plenty of punch.

- 2 tablespoons distilled white vinegar
- 1 tablespoon soy sauce
- 1 tablespoon vegetable oil
- ½ cup coarsely chopped onion
- 1 garlic clove, chopped
- ½ teaspoon ground allspice
- ¼ teaspoon freshly grated nutmeg
- ¼ teaspoon cinnamon
- ⅛ teaspoon cayenne
- ½ teaspoon salt
- ¾ pound pork tenderloin, trimmed

Preheat oven to 450° F. and grease a small shallow baking pan.

In a blender blend all ingredients except pork until smooth and transfer to a shallow dish. Add pork, turning to coat well.

Heat a well-seasoned ridged grill pan over moderately high heat until just smoking and grill pork, turning and brushing occasionally with spice paste, until browned well on all sides.

Transfer pork to baking pan and roast until a meat thermometer registers 155° F. for meat that is cooked through but still slightly pink, 5 to 10 minutes. Transfer pork to a cutting board and let stand, loosely covered with foil, 5 minutes.

Cut pork diagonally into ½-inch-thick slices. Serves 2. May be doubled.

Photo on front jacket

KIELBASA, CABBAGE, AND SWEET POTATO STEW

Stews make ideal one-pot meals, but generally take hours to cook. Ours combines the sweet-and-sour flavors of sweet potatoes and cabbage that are cut small to cook fast. To save time, slice cabbage in a food processor with a shredding disk.

      1 tablespoon vegetable oil
    ¾ pound *kielbasa*, cut into
        1-inch pieces
      4 cups thinly sliced cabbage
      1 onion, sliced thin
      1 bay leaf
    ½ teaspoon caraway seeds
      2 cups water
    ¾ pound sweet potatoes
      1 tablespoon red-wine vinegar, or
        to taste

In a large heavy skillet heat oil over moderate heat until hot but not smoking and brown *kielbasa*. Add cabbage, onion, bay leaf, and caraway seeds and cook, stirring occasionally, until cabbage is browned. Add water and simmer, partially covered, 15 minutes. Peel sweet potatoes and cut into ½-inch cubes. Stir sweet potatoes into cabbage mixture and cook, partially covered, 10 minutes, or until sweet potatoes are tender. Stir in vinegar and salt and pepper to taste. Serves 2 generously. May be doubled.

SAUSAGE, PEPPER, AND ONION KEBABS

If you don't have the time to soak wooden skewers for our kebabs, use metal ones. Just be careful, as they get very hot under the broiler.

    ¾ pound sweet Italian sausage, cut
        crosswise into 1½-inch pieces
      1 red bell pepper, cut into
        1½-inch pieces
      1 large onion, cut into 8 wedges and
        separated into pieces
      6 6-inch wooden skewers, soaked in
        water 15 minutes
      2 tablespoons red-wine vinegar
    ¼ teaspoon dried thyme, crumbled
    ¼ teaspoon dried rosemary, crumbled
    ¼ teaspoon dried oregano, crumbled
    ¼ cup vegetable oil

Alternately thread sausage, bell pepper, and onion onto skewers and arrange in one layer in a shallow baking dish.

In a small bowl whisk together vinegar, herbs, and salt and pepper to taste and add oil in a stream, whisking until combined well. Pour marinade over kebabs, turning to coat, and marinate 20 minutes.

Preheat broiler.

Transfer kebabs to rack of a broiler pan, reserving marinade, and broil about 6 inches from heat, turning twice, until browned on all sides, about 8 minutes.

While kebabs are broiling, transfer reserved marinade to a small saucepan and boil 1 minute.

Serve kebabs drizzled with marinade. Serves 2. May be doubled.

Vietnamese-Style Grilled Steak with Noodles

This flavorful, pretty dish is ideal for both family and guests—It's quick to prepare, low in fat and calories, and you'll have many of the ingredients on hand in your pantry. Cooking the flank steak on an outdoor grill adds charcoal flavor, but when you're in a hurry, use your stovetop grill pan. Cut the steak into thin, wide slices by slicing across the grain with a knife held at a 45-degree angle to the cutting board. This cuts the meat fibers for more tender steak.

    4 ounces *capellini*
For sauce
  2½ tablespoons white-wine vinegar
    1 tablespoon plus 1 teaspoon soy sauce
    1 garlic clove, minced
    1 tablespoon water
    1 tablespoon sugar
   ¼ teaspoon salt
   ⅛ teaspoon dried hot red pepper flakes
   ⅛ teaspoon anchovy paste

   ¼ cup packed fresh mint leaves, shredded, or 1 teaspoon dried mint, crumbled
   ½ pound trimmed flank steak
   ½ cup fresh bean sprouts, rinsed and drained
    1 small red bell pepper, cut into julienne strips (about 1 cup)

Garnish: 2 fresh mint sprigs

Prepare grill. Bring a large saucepan of salted water to a boil for noodles.

Cook noodles in boiling water until just tender and drain in a colander. Rinse noodles under cold water and drain well.
Make sauce:

In a blender blend sauce ingredients until smooth.

In a large bowl toss noodles with sauce and mint. Pat steak dry and season with salt and pepper. Grill steak on an oiled rack set 4 to 5 inches over glowing coals 3 minutes on each side, or until springy to the touch, for medium-rare. (Alternatively, grill steak in a hot well-seasoned ridged grill pan over moderately high heat in same manner.) Transfer steak to a cutting board and let stand 5 minutes.

Cut steak against grain into thin slices. Divide noodles between 2 plates, mounding them, and top with steak. Arrange bean sprouts and bell pepper around noodles and garnish with mint sprigs. Serves 2. May be doubled.

Photo opposite

Each serving: 453 calories, 10 grams fat (20% of calories from fat)

BEEF GOULASH WITH RED BELL PEPPERS

> 2　6-ounce filets mignons, cut into 1-inch cubes
> 2　tablespoons all-purpose flour seasoned with salt and pepper
> 2　tablespoons olive oil
> 2　cups chopped onion
> 1　red bell pepper, sliced thin
> 2　teaspoons paprika, or to taste
> ½　cup dry red wine
> ½　cup beef broth
> ¼　cup sour cream

Accompaniment: cooked egg noodles

Garnish: about 2 tablespoons minced fresh parsley leaves

In a bowl toss beef with seasoned flour to coat. In a heavy skillet heat oil over moderately high heat until hot but not smoking and brown beef. Transfer beef with a slotted spoon to another bowl and in fat remaining in skillet cook onion and bell pepper over moderate heat, stirring occasionally, until onion is golden brown. Stir in paprika and cook, stirring, 1 minute. Add wine and simmer, stirring, 1 minute. Stir in broth, sour cream, and salt and pepper to taste and simmer, stirring occasionally, 5 minutes. Stir in beef and juices that have accumulated in bowl and cook just until beef is heated through, about 1 minute. (Do not overcook meat or it will toughen.)

Serve goulash over noodles and sprinkle with parsley. Serves 2 generously. May be doubled.

CHILI WON TON TRIANGLES WITH SPICY SALSA

For salsa
> 3　vine-ripened tomatoes, seeded and chopped
> 1½　pickled *jalapeños*, seeded and minced
> 3　tablespoons minced fresh coriander sprigs
> 2　tablespoons fresh lime juice

For won ton filling
> ¼　pound ground chuck
> 2　tablespoons minced onion
> ½　teaspoon minced garlic
> ½　teaspoon chili powder
> ¼　teaspoon dried oregano, crumbled
> ¼　cup rinsed drained canned kidney beans
> ¼　cup grated Monterey Jack

> 12　won ton wrappers, thawed if frozen, covered with a dampened kitchen towel

Make salsa:

In a small bowl stir together salsa ingredients.

Bring a kettle of salted water to a gentle boil for won tons.

Make won ton filling:

In a skillet cook chuck, onion, garlic, chili powder, and oregano over moderate heat, stirring and breaking up lumps, until meat is no longer pink and transfer with a slotted spoon to a bowl. In a small bowl with a fork mash 2 tablespoons beans and add to chuck mixture with remaining 2 tablespoons beans, Monterey Jack, and salt and pepper to taste.

Arrange 1 won ton wrapper on a lightly-floured work surface with a corner facing you and moisten edge. Mound 2 rounded teaspoons filling in center. Fold corner facing you over filling to form a triangle and pinch edges together, pressing out any air bubbles and sealing edges well. Make more won ton triangles with remaining wrappers and filling in same manner.

Cook won tons in gently boiling water until just tender, about 8 minutes, and drain in a colander.

Serve won tons topped with salsa. Makes 12 won tons, serving 2. May be doubled.

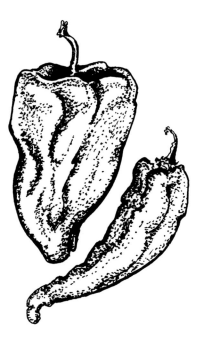

CUMIN LAMB BURGERS IN PITA POCKETS

Kibbeh (Middle Eastern lamb patties) traditionally are made with bulgur, but here we've substituted oatmeal to speed up our recipe. The oatmeal also lightens the lamb mixture, making the patties juicier.

  3 tablespoons old-fashioned rolled oats
  1 tablespoon grated onion
  1 tablespoon cold water
  ½ teaspoon ground cumin
  ½ pound ground lamb
  2 6- to 7-inch pita loaves

Accompaniments: vine-ripened tomato slices, onion slices, lettuce leaves, and bottled mint sauce (such as Crosse & Blackwell)

In a small food processor or blender purée oats, onion, water, cumin, and salt and pepper to taste until a paste forms. In a bowl combine well oat mixture and lamb and form into two 1-inch-thick patties. Brush a well-seasoned ridged grill pan or cast-iron skillet with oil and heat over moderately high heat until it just begins to smoke. Add patties and cook, covered, 3 minutes on each side for medium-rare.

Cut a 1-inch slice off each pita to open pocket. Stuff loaves with patties, tomato, onion, and lettuce and drizzle with mint sauce. Serves 2. May be doubled.

BROILED LAMB CHOPS WITH EGGPLANT AND TOMATO SALAD

While most eggplant salads call for roasting or grilling whole eggplants (a time-consuming procedure), we've broiled eggplant cubes for a delicious smoky flavor in minutes.

¾ pound eggplant, peeled and cut into 1-inch cubes (about 3 cups)
3 tablespoons olive oil
1 vine-ripened tomato, seeded and chopped
2 teaspoons fresh lemon juice, or to taste
¼ teaspoon minced garlic
1½ teaspoons chopped fresh rosemary leaves or ½ teaspoon dried rosemary, crumbled
4 1¼-inch-thick loin lamb chops (about 1 pound total)

Preheat broiler.

In a bowl toss eggplant with oil and salt and pepper to taste and spread on a baking sheet. Broil eggplant about 4 inches from heat, turning occasionally, until golden and tender, about 10 minutes. In a bowl stir together eggplant, tomato, lemon juice, garlic, rosemary, and salt and pepper to taste and let stand while broiling chops.

Season lamb chops with salt and pepper and on oiled rack of broiler pan broil about 4 inches from heat 3 to 4 minutes on each side for medium-rare.

Serve lamb chops with eggplant salad. Serves 2. May be doubled.

RACK OF LAMB WITH CARAMELIZED SHALLOT AND THYME CRUST

Rack of lamb has always been an ideal choice for entertaining—it is quick to prepare and elegant. Have your butcher "french" the bones (remove all meat and fat) for a special gourmet look.

1½ tablespoons olive oil
3 large shallots, chopped (about ½ cup)
3 tablespoons balsamic vinegar
½ cup fine fresh bread crumbs
1½ tablespoons chopped fresh thyme leaves or 2 teaspoons dried thyme, crumbled
1 frenched rack of lamb (7 or 8 ribs) at room temperature, trimmed of fat
1 teaspoon Dijon mustard

Preheat oven to 400° F.

In a small skillet heat oil over moderate heat until hot but not smoking and cook shallots with salt and pepper to taste, stirring, until golden, about 5 minutes. Add vinegar and boil until liquid is evaporated. Remove skillet from heat and stir in bread crumbs, thyme, and salt and pepper to taste.

Season lamb with salt and pepper and arrange, ribs side down, in a small roasting pan. Spread meat side with mustard and pat on crumb mixture evenly. Roast lamb in middle of oven until a meat thermometer registers 135° F. for medium-rare, 25 to 30 minutes. Carefully transfer lamb to a cutting board and let stand 5 minutes.

Slice lamb into chops. Serves 2 generously. May be doubled.

Photo opposite

Rack of Lamb with Caramelized Shallot and Thyme Crust; Stir-fried Spinach with Ginger and Garlic (page 159); and Gruyère Potato Gratin (page 155)

Veal Scaloppine with Mushroom Wine Sauce

¾ pound veal scallops
    (about ⅛ inch thick)
3   tablespoons olive oil
¼   cup finely chopped onion
1   large garlic clove, minced
¼   pound mushrooms, sliced
1   tablespoon white-wine vinegar
½   cup dry white wine
¼   cup water
¼   teaspoon dried tarragon,
    crumbled
½   teaspoon cornstarch dissolved in
    1 tablespoon hot water

*Garnish: about 1 tablespoon minced fresh
parsley leaves*

Pat veal scallops dry and season with salt and pepper. In a large heavy skillet heat 2 tablespoons oil over moderately high heat until hot but not smoking and sauté veal in batches until golden brown and just cooked through, about 30 seconds on each side, transferring to a plate.

Add remaining tablespoon oil to skillet and cook onion and garlic over moderately low heat, stirring, until softened, about 3 minutes. Add mushrooms and sauté over moderately high heat, stirring, until liquid mushrooms give off is evaporated. Add vinegar and boil until liquid is evaporated. Add wine, water, and tarragon and boil until liquid is reduced by about half.

Stir cornstarch mixture and add to sauce, stirring until slightly thickened. Add veal and juices that have accumulated on plate and cook over moderately low heat just until heated through, about 1 minute.

Serve veal *scaloppine* sprinkled with parsley. Serves 2. May be doubled.

ZUCCHINI STUFFED WITH CORN, BELL PEPPER, AND VEAL

Corn is often used as a fat-free binder in soups and chowders. Here it also moistens lean veal without the need for eggs or cream.

¾ pound zucchini (about 3 small or 2 medium), halved lengthwise
½ teaspoon olive oil
¼ pound ground veal
½ cup finely chopped red bell pepper
1 garlic clove, minced
2 tablespoons finely chopped shallot
1 cup corn, thawed if frozen
2 tablespoons freshly grated Parmesan
¾ teaspoon freshly grated lemon zest
1 teaspoon Worcestershire sauce, or to taste
1 tablespoon chopped fresh parsley leaves

Preheat oven to 450° F.

On a baking sheet arrange zucchini, cut sides up, and season with salt and pepper. Roast zucchini in middle of oven 20 minutes, or until just tender.

While zucchini is roasting, in a non-stick skillet heat oil over moderate heat until hot but not smoking and cook veal, stirring to break up any lumps, until barely pink. Add bell pepper, garlic, shallot, and ½ cup corn and cook, stirring, until vegetables are just tender. Remove skillet from heat.

Carefully scoop out flesh of zucchini with a spoon, transferring it to a blender and leaving 1/4-inch-thick shells. Purée zucchini flesh with remaining ½ cup corn until smooth. Stir purée into veal mixture with 1 tablespoon Parmesan, zest, Worcestershire sauce, parsley, and salt and pepper to taste. Spoon filling into zucchini shells and sprinkle with remaining tablespoon Parmesan. Bake stuffed zucchini in middle of oven until hot and cheese is melted, about 1 minute. Serves 2 as an entrée. May be doubled.

Each serving: 252 calories, 8 grams fat, (29% of calories from fat)

GRILLED CHICKEN BREASTS STUFFED WITH HAM AND SAGA BLUE CHEESE

1   whole boneless chicken breast with skin (about ¾ pound), halved
2   sticks Saga Blue cheese without rind (each about 2 by ½ by ½ inch)
2   thin slices cooked ham (each about 4 by 4 inches)
1   tablespoon Worcestershire sauce
1   tablespoon fresh lemon juice
2   tablespoons unsalted butter, cut into pieces

Prepare grill.

Insert a sharp paring knife into thicker end of each chicken breast half and cut a lengthwise pocket carefully, making it as wide as possible without puncturing sides. Wrap each cheese stick in a ham slice, enclosing it, and insert packages in chicken pockets. Seal each opening well with a toothpick and season chicken with salt and pepper. In a small saucepan bring Worcestershire sauce and lemon juice just to a simmer. Remove pan from heat and swirl in butter.

Grill chicken on an oiled rack set about 6 inches over glowing coals, basting frequently with sauce, 12 minutes on each side, or until cooked through. (Do not baste chicken during last 2 minutes of grilling and discard any unused sauce.) Serves 2. May be doubled.

Photo opposite

CHILI CORNMEAL CHICKEN WINGS

10   chicken wings (about 2 pounds), tips discarded and wings halved at joint
½   cup plain yogurt
¼   cup cornmeal
¼   cup dry bread crumbs
2   teaspoons chili powder
½   teaspoon ground cumin
½   teaspoon salt
⅛   teaspoon cayenne

Preheat oven to 425° F. and line a baking pan with foil.

In a small bowl toss wings with yogurt until coated. In another bowl stir together remaining ingredients and dredge wings in mixture, arranging them in pan in one layer.

Bake wings in middle of oven, turning them halfway through baking, 30 minutes, or until browned. Serves 2. May be doubled.

Grilled Chicken Breasts Stuffed with Ham and Saga Blue Cheese; Celery and Apple Salad Dijon (page 165)

ORANGE AND ROSEMARY GLAZED CORNISH HENS

To split each Cornish hen, cut out the backbone with poultry shears from the tail end to the neck end by snipping through the ribs on either side of the backbone. Then, turn the hen over on a work surface, bone side down, and press firmly on the breastbone to flatten it.

⅓ cup frozen orange juice concentrate
2 tablespoons fresh lemon juice
¾ teaspoon dried rosemary, crumbled
¾ teaspoon black pepper
2 1¼- to 1½-pound Cornish hens, halved and backbones discarded

Preheat oven to 500° F. and line a baking pan with foil.

In a saucepan heat concentrate, lemon juice, rosemary, and pepper over moderately low heat until concentrate is melted. Pat hens dry and season with salt and pepper. Arrange hens, skin sides down, in baking pan and brush with some orange mixture.

Roast hens in middle of oven, turning hens after 15 minutes and basting occasionally with orange mixture, until juices run clear when fleshy part of a thigh is pierced, about 30 minutes. (Do not baste hens during last 2 minutes of roasting and discard any unused orange mixture.) Serves 2. May be doubled.

SPANISH-STYLE CHICKEN WITH OLIVES AND RICE

To quickly cut up canned tomatoes right in the can, drain the tomatoes, then use kitchen scissors to snip them into small pieces.

2 pounds chicken legs, thighs, and/or wings with skin
2 tablespoons olive oil
1 small onion, chopped
1 garlic clove, minced
½ cup long-grain white rice
¼ cup dry white wine
1 cup chicken broth
1 14-ounce can whole tomatoes, drained and chopped
1 teaspoon paprika
¼ teaspoon crumbled saffron threads
½ cup pitted whole green olives
1 tablespoon minced fresh parsley leaves

Pat chicken dry and season with salt and pepper. In a large heavy skillet heat oil over moderately high heat until hot but not smoking and brown chicken, transferring to a plate. Pour off all but about 1 tablespoon fat from skillet and cook onion and garlic over moderately low heat, stirring, 2 minutes. Add rice, wine, broth, tomatoes, paprika, saffron, olives, and salt and pepper to taste and bring liquid to a boil. Add chicken with any juices that have accumulated on plate and simmer, covered, 20 minutes, or until liquid is absorbed and chicken cooked through. Sprinkle chicken with parsley. Serves 2. May be doubled.

CHICKEN THIGHS WITH CURRIED TOMATO SAUCE AND RICE

1 cup water
⅓ cup long-grain white rice
1 tablespoon all-purpose flour
2 teaspoons curry powder
1½ cups canned whole tomatoes including juice
1 small onion, chopped fine
2 tablespoons bottled mango chutney
1 tablespoon fresh lemon juice
4 chicken thighs (about ¾ pound), skin and fat discarded
1 tablespoon chopped fresh parsley leaves

In a small saucepan bring water to a boil and stir in rice and salt to taste. Simmer rice, covered, over moderately low heat, until water is absorbed, about 20 minutes.

While rice is simmering, in a heavy 10-inch skillet cook flour and curry powder over moderately low heat, stirring constantly, until fragrant, about 2 minutes. Add tomatoes with juice, onion, chutney, and lemon juice, stirring to break up tomatoes. Add chicken thighs and simmer over moderate heat, covered, turning chicken halfway through simmering, 15 minutes. Stir in parsley and simmer, uncovered, 2 minutes, or until sauce is slightly thickened and chicken is cooked through.

Serve chicken and sauce over rice. Serves 2. May be doubled.

Each serving: 407 calories, 7 grams fat (15% of calories from fat)

CHICKEN AND SHALLOTS WITH RIESLING AND GRAPES

This dish is especially delicious when prepared with a fruity California or German Riesling, although any dry white wine will do.

1 whole chicken breast with skin and bones (about 1 pound), halved
4 shallots, peeled and halved
1 tablespoon unsalted butter, softened
¼ teaspoon dried thyme, crumbled
½ lemon
2 teaspoons all-purpose flour
⅓ cup Riesling
½ cup chicken broth
¼ pound green seedless grapes, halved crosswise (about ¾ cup)

Preheat oven to 400° F.

Arrange chicken, skin sides up, in an ovenproof skillet and scatter shallots around it. Spread butter on chicken and sprinkle with thyme and salt and pepper to taste. Squeeze juice of ½ lemon over chicken and bake in upper third of oven 35 minutes, or until cooked through. Transfer chicken with tongs to a heated platter and keep warm, covered.

Whisk flour into pan juices and whisk in Riesling. Boil mixture, whisking, 1 minute and add broth and grapes. Boil sauce, stirring, 3 minutes, or until slightly thickened, and pour over chicken. Serves 2. May be doubled.

CHICKEN AND SAUSAGE COUSCOUS

1 small onion, chopped fine
2 tablespoons unsalted butter
½ teaspoon turmeric
¼ teaspoon dried hot
    red pepper flakes
2 teaspoons tomato paste
1½ cups chicken broth
¾ cup water
3 chicken wings, tips discarded and
    wings halved at joint
½ pound *kielbasa*, cut diagonally into
    ½-inch-thick slices
1 carrot, cut diagonally into
    ½-inch-thick slices
1 turnip, peeled and cut into
    ½-inch-thick wedges
1 3-inch cinnamon stick
½ bay leaf
½ cup rinsed drained canned
    chick-peas
¾ cup couscous

In a saucepan cook onion in 1 tablespoon butter over moderately low heat, stirring, until softened. Add turmeric and red pepper flakes and cook, stirring, 1 minute. Stir in tomato paste, broth, water, chicken, *kielbasa*, carrot, turnip, cinnamon stick, and ½ bay leaf and simmer, covered, 20 minutes, or until vegetables are tender. Add chick-peas and simmer 5 minutes.

Strain 1 cup cooking liquid through a sieve into a small saucepan and add remaining tablespoon butter. Bring mixture to a boil and stir in couscous. Remove pan from heat and let couscous stand, covered, 5 minutes. Fluff couscous with a fork.

Divide couscous between 2 plates and make a well in center of each serving. Transfer meat and vegetables with a slotted spoon to wells, discarding ½ bay leaf, and serve remaining broth separately. Serves 2. May be doubled.

Photo opposite

PAN-GRILLED CHICKEN WITH ALMOND SAUCE

¼ cup whole almonds
¼ cup chicken broth
2 tablespoons chopped fresh
    parsley leaves
1 tablespoon fresh lemon juice
½ teaspoon dried oregano,
    crumbled
½ teaspoon sugar
1 garlic clove, chopped
3 tablespoons extra-virgin olive oil
1 large whole boneless chicken breast
    with skin (about 1 pound), halved

In a food processor or blender grind almonds fine. Add broth, parsley, juice, oregano, sugar, and garlic and blend until smooth. With motor running add oil in a stream and season sauce with salt and pepper.

Pat chicken dry and season with salt and pepper. Heat an oiled well-seasoned ridged grill pan or cast-iron skillet over moderately high heat until oil just begins to smoke and grill chicken, skin sides down, covered, turning halfway through grilling, 10 minutes, or until just cooked through. Transfer chicken to a cutting board and let stand 5 minutes.

Cut chicken lengthwise into thin slices. Divide chicken between 2 plates and drizzle with sauce. Serves 2. May be doubled.

ASIAN-SPICED CHICKEN BREASTS

To quickly crush anise seeds or other spices, use a mortar and pestle or the back of a heavy skillet.

1½ tablespoons soy sauce
1 tablespoon Scotch or medium-dry Sherry
1 teaspoon minced peeled fresh gingerroot
½ teaspoon sugar
1 tablespoon cornstarch
¼ teaspoon anise seeds, crushed
⅛ teaspoon cinnamon
¾ cup water
1 large whole boneless chicken breast with skin (about 1 pound), halved
1 tablespoon vegetable oil
1 scallion, minced

In a small saucepan bring soy sauce, Scotch or Sherry, gingerroot, sugar, ½ teaspoon cornstarch, anise, cinnamon, and water to a boil, whisking, and simmer sauce, covered, 5 minutes.

While sauce is simmering, pat chicken dry and rub both sides with remaining 2½ teaspoons cornstarch, shaking off excess. In a large non-stick skillet heat oil over moderately high heat until it just begins to smoke and sear chicken, skin sides down, pressing with a metal spatula to flatten, 4 minutes, or until golden brown. Turn chicken. Strain soy sauce mixture through a fine sieve into skillet and simmer 10 minutes, covered, or until chicken is just cooked through. Transfer chicken, skin sides up, with a slotted spatula to plates and simmer sauce, stirring, 1 minute, or until slightly thickened.

Spoon sauce around chicken and sprinkle with scallion. Serves 2. May be doubled.

CHICKEN CUTLETS WITH GINGER, SCALLION, AND GARLIC

1 whole skinless boneless chicken breast (about ¾ pound), halved
2 tablespoons soy sauce
3 tablespoons vegetable oil
2 teaspoons minced peeled fresh gingerroot
⅓ cup thinly sliced scallions
1 garlic clove, minced
1 tablespoon fresh lemon juice

Halve chicken pieces horizontally with a sharp knife and flatten to ⅓-inch-thick cutlets between sheets of plastic wrap. In a shallow dish whisk together soy sauce, 1 tablespoon oil, and pepper to taste. Add chicken, turning to coat, and marinate, covered and chilled, 15 minutes.

Drain chicken and pat dry. In a large heavy skillet heat 1 tablespoon oil over moderately high heat until hot but not smoking and sauté chicken 1 minute on each side, or until browned and cooked through. Transfer chicken with tongs to a platter and keep warm, covered loosely. To skillet add remaining tablespoon oil, gingerroot, scallions, and garlic and cook, stirring, 1 minute. Stir in lemon juice and spoon sauce over chicken. Serves 2. May be doubled.

GRANDÉ CHICKEN AND BLACK BEAN BURRITOS

While flour tortillas are available (fresh or frozen) in many supermarkets, outstanding fresh tortillas with homemade flavor can be mail-ordered from Maria and Ricardo's Tortilla Factory in Jamaica Plain, Massachusetts, tel. (617) 524-6107.

　1　teaspoon vegetable oil
　1　small whole skinless boneless chicken breast (about $\frac{1}{2}$ pound), cut into $\frac{1}{2}$-inch pieces
$\frac{1}{2}$　red bell pepper, cut into $\frac{1}{2}$-inch pieces
　1　scallion, sliced thin
　1　teaspoon ground cumin
$\frac{1}{8}$　teaspoon dried hot red pepper flakes
$\frac{3}{4}$　cup rinsed drained canned black beans
$\frac{1}{2}$　cup canned whole tomatoes including juice
　2　tablespoons chopped fresh coriander sprigs
　2　10-inch flour tortillas

Accompaniment: $\frac{1}{4}$ cup salsa

In a heavy non-stick skillet heat oil over moderately high heat until hot but not smoking and sauté chicken, bell pepper, scallion, and salt and pepper to taste, stirring occasionally, until chicken is just cooked through, about 5 minutes. Add cumin and red pepper flakes and cook, stirring, 1 minute. Add beans, tomatoes with juice, and coriander, stirring to break up tomatoes, and simmer until most of liquid is evaporated.

In a saucepan on a rack set over $\frac{1}{2}$ inch of simmering water steam tortillas, covered, until soft and pliable, about 30 seconds.

Arrange 1 tortilla on work surface and mound half of chicken mixture on lower half of tortilla, leaving a $\frac{1}{2}$-inch border along edge. Roll up filling tightly in tortilla, folding in sides after first roll to completely enclose filling, and continue rolling. Make another burrito with remaining tortilla and filling in same manner.

Serve salsa spooned over burritos. Serves 2. May be doubled.

Each serving: 492 calories, 11 grams fat (20% of calories from fat)

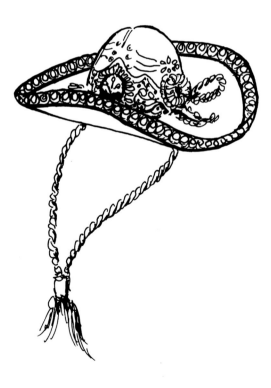

LEMON CHICKEN AND ROASTED PEPPER SANDWICHES

If you can't find arugula for our sandwiches, substitute watercress, which also has a peppery, mustard-flavored bite.

1 whole skinless boneless chicken breast (about ¾ pound), halved
1 tablespoon fresh lemon juice
1 tablespoon all-purpose flour
½ teaspoon fennel seeds, crushed
1 tablespoon olive oil
⅓ cup drained bottled roasted red peppers, cut into thin strips
2 kaiser rolls, split and toasted
1 small bunch arugula, washed well and spun dry

In a bowl coat chicken with lemon juice and marinate, turning once, 10 minutes.

On a sheet of wax paper stir together flour, fennel seeds, and salt and pepper to taste. Remove chicken from bowl, letting excess lemon juice drip into bowl and reserving it, and dredge chicken in flour mixture, shaking off excess.

In a 10-inch non-stick skillet heat oil over moderately high heat until hot but not smoking and sauté chicken about 3 minutes, or until lightly browned. Turn chicken and cook over moderate heat 5 minutes, or until cooked through. Transfer chicken to a cutting board. To skillet add roasted pepper and reserved lemon juice and simmer until most of liquid is evaporated, about 2 minutes.

Slice chicken thin. Make sandwiches on rolls with arugula, chicken, and roasted pepper. Serves 2. May be doubled.

Photo opposite

SAUTÉED CHICKEN WITH PEAR AND CIDER SAUCE

1 small whole skinless boneless chicken breast (about ½ pound), cut into 2-inch pieces
1 teaspoon vegetable oil
1 red onion, cut into ½-inch-thick slices
1 firm-ripe Bosc pear
½ cup apple cider
1 teaspoon all-purpose flour
1 teaspoon cider vinegar
½ teaspoon dried thyme leaves, crumbled

Pat chicken dry and season with salt and pepper. In a non-stick skillet heat oil over moderately high heat until hot but not smoking and sauté chicken and onion, stirring, until chicken is golden and almost cooked through, about 4 minutes. Core pear and cut into 1-inch pieces. In a 1-cup measure stir together cider and flour and add to chicken mixture. Stir in pear, vinegar, and thyme and simmer until pear is tender, chicken is cooked through, and sauce is slightly thickened, about 3 minutes. Serves 2. May be doubled.

Each serving: 243 calories, 4 grams fat (15% of calories from fat)

CRISP COCONUT CHICKEN NUGGETS WITH SPICY SWEET-AND-SOUR SAUCE

½ red bell pepper, chopped coarse
½ cup distilled white vinegar
⅓ cup sugar
½ teaspoon dried hot red pepper flakes
all-purpose flour seasoned with salt and pepper for dredging
1 large egg beaten with 1 teaspoon water
1 cup sweetened flaked coconut
1 whole skinless boneless chicken breast (about ¾ pound), cut into 1½-inch pieces
2 tablespoons vegetable oil

In a blender purée bell pepper with vinegar and transfer to a small saucepan. Stir in sugar, red pepper flakes, and salt to taste and simmer 5 minutes. Remove pan from heat and cool sauce.

In 3 separate bowls have ready seasoned flour; egg mixture; and coconut. Dredge chicken in flour and dip each piece in egg mixture, letting excess drip off. Coat each piece thoroughly with coconut, pressing to make it adhere.

In a large skillet heat oil over moderate heat until hot but not smoking and cook coated chicken 3 minutes on each side, or until crisp and browned.

Serve dipping sauce on the side. Serves 2. May be doubled.

PROSCIUTTO AND SPINACH STUFFED TURKEY CUTLETS

2 4-ounce turkey breast cutlets, lightly pounded
2 thin slices prosciutto (about 1 ounce), excess fat trimmed
½ cup packed spinach leaves, washed well and spun dry
3 teaspoons all-purpose flour
2 teaspoons vegetable oil
1 shallot, sliced thin
½ cup chicken broth
2 tablespoons dry white wine
1 tablespoon chopped fresh basil leaves
2 teaspoons fresh lemon juice
½ teaspoon freshly grated lemon zest

Arrange turkey cutlets on a work surface and top each with a prosciutto slice. Arrange spinach leaves over prosciutto and fold each turkey cutlet crosswise in half. Sprinkle cutlets with 2 teaspoons flour and season with salt and pepper.

In a non-stick skillet heat oil over moderately high heat until hot but not smoking and sauté cutlets and shallot until turkey is golden and almost cooked through, about 4 minutes on each side. In a 1-cup measure stir together chicken broth and remaining teaspoon flour and add to turkey mixture with remaining ingredients and salt and pepper to taste. Simmer mixture until turkey is cooked through and sauce is slightly thickened, about 2 minutes. Serves 2. May be doubled.

Each serving: 265 calories, 9 grams fat (30% of calories from fat)

TURKEY BURGERS WITH CURRIED MAYONNAISE AND SPINACH

1   small garlic clove, minced and mashed to a paste with ¼ teaspoon salt
3   tablespoons mayonnaise
¾   teaspoon curry powder
1   tablespoon minced bottled sweet pickle
¾   pound ground turkey
2   tablespoons chopped scallion
2   teaspoons Worcestershire sauce
2   saltine crackers, crushed fine
1   tablespoon vegetable oil
2   English muffins, split and toasted lightly
½   cup packed fresh spinach leaves, washed well and spun dry

In a bowl stir together garlic paste, mayonnaise, curry powder, pickle, and pepper to taste. In another bowl combine well turkey, scallion, Worcestershire sauce, and cracker crumbs and form into two 1-inch-thick patties. Season patties with salt and pepper. In a heavy skillet (preferably cast-iron) heat oil over moderately high heat until hot but not smoking and sauté patties until cooked through, about 6 minutes on each side.

Make sandwiches on muffins with burgers, curried mayonnaise, and spinach leaves. Serves 2. May be doubled.

TURKEY PASTRAMI REUBEN

Spicy turkey pastrami, a much leaner version than smoked beef pastrami, is becoming a popular deli item. However, if you can't find it, you can mail-order it from Nodine's Smokehouse, Torrington, Connecticut, tel. (800) 222-2059.

2   ½-inch-thick slices nonfat peasant-style bread
1½   tablespoons Dijon mustard
4   ounces packaged sauerkraut, rinsed well and drained well
¼   pound thinly sliced turkey pastrami
2   tablespoons grated Swiss cheese (about ½ ounce)

Preheat broiler.

Arrange bread on a baking sheet and spread mustard on top of each. Top each slice with one fourth of sauerkraut and divide pastrami and remaining sauerkraut between slices. Sprinkle tops with cheese and broil about 4 inches from heat until cheese is melted, about 1 minute. Serves 2. May be doubled.

Each serving: 248 calories, 7 grams fat (25% of calories from fat)

BREAKFASTS & BRUNCHES

Breakfast Dishes

BAKED PEAR PANCAKE WITH GINGERED MAPLE SYRUP

Making one large puffy pancake is easier (and more impressive) than making many smaller ones. If the handle of your skillet isn't ovenproof, wrap it in several layers of aluminum foil.

    2½ tablespoons granulated sugar
    ½   teaspoon cinnamon
    2   ripe small pears (about ¾ pound)
    2   teaspoons fresh lemon juice
    ½   cup all-purpose flour
    2   large eggs
    ⅓   cup milk
    2   tablespoons unsalted butter
For syrup
    ½   cup pure maple syrup
    2   tablespoons water
    1   tablespoon fresh lemon juice
    1   tablespoon firmly packed light
        brown sugar
    2   teaspoons minced crystallized
        ginger
    ¼   cup raisins

Garnish: confectioners' sugar

Accompaniment: sour cream

Preheat oven to 450° F.

In a cup stir together granulated sugar and cinnamon. Peel pears and quarter them lengthwise. Core pear quarters and slice thin crosswise. In a bowl toss pears with 2 teaspoons lemon juice and 1 tablespoon cinnamon sugar. In another bowl whisk together flour, 1 tablespoon cinnamon sugar, and a pinch salt. In a small bowl whisk together eggs and milk and add to flour mixture in a stream, whisking until just combined (batter will be slightly lumpy).

In a well-seasoned 9-inch cast-iron skillet heat 1 tablespoon butter over moderate heat, rotating skillet to coat, until foam subsides. Pour batter into skillet and sprinkle evenly with pear mixture. Cook pancake 3 minutes, or until underside is just set. Transfer skillet to middle of oven and bake pancake 10 minutes.

Make syrup while pancake is baking:

In a small saucepan bring all syrup ingredients except raisins to a boil, stirring until sugar is dissolved, and simmer 5 minutes. Add raisins and simmer 1 minute more. Remove gingered syrup from heat and keep warm, covered.

Sprinkle pear pancake with remaining cinnamon sugar and dot with remaining tablespoon butter. Bake pancake 8 minutes more, or until puffed and golden.

Sift confectioners' sugar over pancake and serve immediately with gingered syrup and sour cream. Serves 2.

Photo on page 127

Spicy Smoked Salmon Corn Cakes (page 132)

RAISIN BRAN PANCAKES WITH CIDER SYRUP

Bran, a part of many grains, is the layer richest in fiber, vitamins, and minerals. Wheat or oat bran, available in natural foods stores and most supermarkets, can be used in this recipe.

1¼ cups buttermilk
½ cup bran
⅓ cup raisins
⅔ cup apple cider
¼ cup pure maple syrup
1 cinnamon stick
1 large egg, beaten lightly
2 tablespoons firmly packed light brown sugar
2 tablespoons vegetable oil plus additional for brushing griddle
¾ cup all-purpose flour
1 teaspoon baking soda
½ teaspoon salt

In a bowl whisk together 1 cup buttermilk, bran, and raisins and let stand 15 minutes.

In a small heavy saucepan boil cider, maple syrup, and cinnamon stick, stirring occasionally, until thickened and reduced by about one third. Remove pan from heat and keep cider syrup warm, covered.

In a large bowl whisk together egg and brown sugar and whisk in 2 tablespoons oil, raisin bran mixture, and remaining ¼ cup buttermilk. Into mixture sift together flour, baking soda, and salt and stir until well combined.

Preheat oven to 200° F.

Heat a griddle over moderate heat until hot enough to make drops of water scatter over its surface and brush with additional oil. Working in batches, drop pancake batter by ¼-cup measures onto griddle and cook 1 to 2 minutes on each side, or until golden and cooked through. Transfer pancakes as cooked to a heatproof platter and keep warm, uncovered, in oven.

Discard cinnamon stick and serve pancakes with cider syrup. Makes about twelve 4-inch pancakes, serving 2.

CINNAMON RAISIN OATMEAL WITH HONEY CREAM

2 tablespoons heavy cream at room temperature
2 tablespoons honey
2 cups cold water
1 cup old-fashioned oats
3 tablespoons golden raisins
¼ teaspoon cinnamon, or to taste
¼ teaspoon salt, if desired

In a small bowl stir together cream and honey. In a small saucepan stir together remaining ingredients. Bring oat mixture to a boil and simmer, stirring occasionally, 5 minutes.

Serve oatmeal drizzled with honey cream. Serves 2. May be doubled.

Baked Pear Pancake with Gingered Maple Syrup (page 125)

CURRIED POTATO AND EGG HASH

1 medium russet (baking) potato,
  peeled and cut into ½-inch cubes
1 whole large egg
3 large egg whites
½ cup thinly sliced scallions
½ tablespoon unsalted butter
½ teaspoon curry powder, or to taste

In a saucepan of boiling salted water cook potato until just tender, about 5 minutes. While potatoes are cooking, in a bowl whisk together whole egg and whites, scallions, and salt and pepper to taste. Drain potatoes in a sieve.

In a non-stick skillet heat butter over moderately high heat until foam subsides and sauté potato, stirring, until golden. Reduce heat to moderately low. Add curry powder and cook, stirring, 30 seconds. Add eggs and cook, stirring occasionally, until just cooked through. Serves 2. May be doubled.

Each serving: 235 calories, 6 grams fat
(23% of calories from fat)

BANANA GINGER WAFFLES

Our waffles are made in a 7-inch waffle iron—if yours is a different size, adjust the amount of batter accordingly. Be sure to spray your waffle iron with a light coating of vegetable cooking spray before heating. You won't need to spray it again between batches.

vegetable-oil cooking spray
2   ripe bananas (about 12 ounces total)
1   large egg, beaten lightly
2   teaspoons unsalted butter, melted and cooled
1½ teaspoons minced peeled fresh gingerroot
⅔   cup all-purpose flour
2   teaspoons baking powder
¼   teaspoon salt
¾   cup fresh seltzer or club soda
2   tablespoons plain low-fat yogurt
2   tablespoons pure maple syrup

Preheat oven to 250° F. Spray a non-stick or a well-seasoned 7-inch round waffle iron lightly with vegetable-oil cooking spray and preheat until hot.

In a small bowl mash enough banana to measure ½ cup and finely chop remaining banana. In a bowl whisk together egg, mashed and chopped bananas, butter, and gingerroot. Into mixture sift together flour, baking powder, and salt. Add seltzer or club soda and stir until just combined.

Pour batter onto waffle iron, using ½ cup batter for a 7-inch round waffle and spreading batter evenly, and cook according to manufacturer's instructions. Transfer waffle to a baking sheet and keep warm, uncovered, in middle of oven. Make more waffles with remaining batter in same manner.

While waffles are cooking, in a small bowl whisk together yogurt and maple syrup.

Serve waffles drizzled with yogurt mixture. Makes four 7-inch round waffles, serving 2.

Each serving: 391 calories, 8 grams fat (18% of calories from fat)

DATE AND WALNUT CARDAMOM MUFFINS

Our muffins have a few sticky ingredients that need special handling: to easily chop the dates, lightly oil the blade of your knife or kitchen scissors; to measure out the honey, lightly oil the measuring cup first.

$1\frac{1}{2}$ cups all-purpose flour
$1\frac{1}{2}$ teaspoons baking powder
$\frac{1}{2}$ teaspoon ground cardamom
$\frac{1}{4}$ teaspoon salt
1 large egg, beaten lightly
$\frac{2}{3}$ cup milk
$\frac{1}{3}$ cup honey
$\frac{1}{2}$ stick ($\frac{1}{4}$ cup) unsalted butter, melted and cooled slightly
$\frac{1}{2}$ cup chopped pitted dates
$\frac{1}{3}$ cup walnuts, lightly toasted and chopped fine

Preheat oven to 375° F. and butter and flour nine $\frac{1}{2}$-cup muffin tins, knocking out excess flour.

Into a bowl sift together flour, baking powder, cardamom, and salt. In another bowl whisk together egg, milk, honey, and butter and stir into flour mixture until just combined. Stir in dates and walnuts. Divide batter among tins and bake in middle of oven 20 minutes, or until a tester comes out clean. Let muffins cool 3 minutes and turn out onto a rack. Makes 9 muffins.

GRANOLA MUFFINS

If your baking powder is more than six months old, test it to make sure that it's still active. Simply add 1 teaspoon of baking powder to $\frac{1}{4}$ cup hot water. If the leavener is still good, the mixture will fizz and bubble.

1 large egg, beaten lightly
$\frac{1}{4}$ cup firmly packed brown sugar
$\frac{1}{2}$ stick ($\frac{1}{4}$ cup) unsalted butter, melted and cooled slightly
$\frac{2}{3}$ cup milk
$\frac{1}{2}$ teaspoon vanilla
1 cup all-purpose flour
$1\frac{1}{2}$ teaspoons baking powder
$\frac{1}{4}$ teaspoon salt
$\frac{3}{4}$ cup granola, large pieces crumbled

Preheat oven to 375° F. and butter seven $\frac{1}{2}$-cup muffin tins.

In a bowl whisk together egg, brown sugar, butter, milk, and vanilla until smooth. Into mixture sift together flour, baking powder, and salt, stirring until just combined. Fold in granola and divide batter among tins. Bake muffins in middle of oven 20 minutes, or until a tester comes out clean. Let muffins cool 3 minutes. Run a knife around each muffin to loosen edge and turn out onto a rack. Makes 7 muffins.

Brunch Dishes

SWEET-POTATO BACON FRITTERS

The key to crispy fritters is making sure that your oil is hot enough and maintaining an even temperature throughout cooking. A deep-fat thermometer is ideal, but if you don't have one, test oil temperature by dropping in a cube of bread; it should brown in 30 to 40 seconds in 375° F. oil.

  4 bacon slices
  1 cup plus 2 tablespoons
     all-purpose flour
  1 teaspoon baking powder
  ½ teaspoon salt
  ⅔ cup milk
  2 large eggs, beaten lightly
  2 tablespoons unsalted butter,
     melted and cooled
  2 cups coarsely grated sweet potato
     vegetable oil for deep-frying

Accompaniment: pure maple syrup

Preheat oven to 250° F. and line a baking sheet with paper towels.

In a skillet cook bacon over moderate heat until crisp and drain on paper towels on a work surface.

Into a bowl sift together flour, baking powder, and salt. Add milk, eggs, and butter and whisk until combined. Crumble bacon and stir into batter with sweet potatoes.

In a deep skillet or deep fryer heat 2 inches of oil to 375° F. Working in batches, fry batter by rounded tablespoons, turning once, 2 minutes, or until golden. Transfer fritters as fried with a slotted spoon to baking sheet and keep warm in oven.

Serve fritters with maple syrup. Serves 2.
Photo opposite

BLUEBERRY AND RASPBERRY COMPOTE WITH BASIL MINT SYRUP

  ½ cup water
  3 tablespoons sugar
  ⅓ cup packed fresh basil leaves,
     washed well and spun dry
  ⅓ cup packed fresh mint leaves,
     washed well and spun dry
  ¾ cup picked-over blueberries
  ¾ cup picked-over raspberries

In a small saucepan boil water and sugar, stirring occasionally, until reduced to about ⅓ cup. Put herbs in a metal bowl. Pour syrup over herbs and steep 5 minutes. Strain syrup through a sieve into a bowl and stir in berries. Serves 2.

Each serving: 131 calories, 1 gram fat
(7% of calories from fat)

KIELBASA HASH BROWNS

¼ pound *kielbasa,* cut into ¼-inch dice
   (about 1 cup)
1 onion, chopped
1 tablespoon vegetable oil
1 large russet (baking) potato, peeled
   and cut into ¼-inch dice

Accompaniment: fried eggs

In a heavy skillet cook *kielbasa* and onion in oil over moderately low heat, stirring, 2 minutes, or until onion begins to soften. Stir in potato and salt and pepper to taste and spread evenly in skillet. Reduce heat to low and cook, covered, 20 minutes. Remove lid and cook hash over moderate heat, stirring, until golden, about 5 minutes.

Serve hash with fried eggs. Serves 2. May be doubled.

SPICY SMOKED SALMON CORN CAKES

¼ cup plus 2 tablespoons yellow
    cornmeal
3 tablespoons all-purpose flour
¼ teaspoon baking soda
¼ teaspoon salt
1 large egg, beaten lightly
3 tablespoons cream cheese, softened
¼ cup plus 2 tablespoons buttermilk
½ cup fresh or frozen corn (thawed
    if frozen)
3 tablespoons finely chopped
    fresh chives
9 large *peperoncini* (pickled Tuscan
    peppers), drained, seeded, and
    chopped fine (about ¼ cup)
2 ounces finely chopped smoked
    salmon (about ⅓ cup)
2 tablespoons vegetable oil

*Accompaniments: sour cream, chopped
red onion, and lemon slices*

In a small bowl whisk together cornmeal, flour, baking soda, and salt. In a bowl whisk together egg and cream cheese and whisk in buttermilk. Chop half of corn coarse and stir into buttermilk mixture with remaining corn, chives, *peperoncini,* salmon, and cornmeal mixture until just combined.

Preheat oven to 200° F.

In a large non-stick skillet heat oil over moderately high heat until hot but not smoking. Working in batches drop batter by ¼-cup measures into skillet, spreading slightly to form 3½- to 4-inch cakes, and cook 2 to 3 minutes on each side, or until golden brown. Transfer corn cakes as cooked to a heatproof platter and keep warm, uncovered, in oven.

Serve corn cakes with sour cream, onion, and lemon. Makes 6 corn cakes, serving 2.
Photo on page 124

PEPPERONI PIZZA FRITTATA

1 small onion, chopped
1 garlic clove, minced
1 tablespoon olive oil
4 large eggs
1 tablespoon tomato paste
1 teaspoon fresh oregano leaves,
    minced, or ¼ teaspoon dried
    oregano, crumbled
2 ounces thinly sliced pepperoni,
    chopped (about ¼ cup)
⅓ cup grated mozzarella (about 2
    ounces)

*Garnish: about 1 tablespoon minced fresh
basil leaves*

In an 8- or 9-inch flameproof heavy skillet cook onion and garlic in oil over moderately low heat, stirring, until softened. In a bowl whisk together eggs, tomato paste, oregano, and pepper to taste and add to onion mixture. Cook eggs, without stirring, 2 minutes. Sprinkle pepperoni evenly over eggs and cook, without stirring, 8 minutes, or until edges are set but center is still soft.

Preheat broiler while *frittata* is cooking.

Sprinkle mozzarella evenly over *frittata* and broil about 4 inches from heat until cheese is bubbling, about 1 minute.

Sprinkle *frittata* with basil and cut into wedges. Serves 2.

GORGONZOLA AND SCALLION SOUFFLÉ

 ½ teaspoon unsalted butter, softened
 1 tablespoon fine fresh bread crumbs
 1 tablespoon tomato paste
 ½ cup skim milk
 1½ tablespoons all-purpose flour
 ½ ounce Gorgonzola cheese (about 1 tablespoon)
 1 garlic clove, minced
 ½ teaspoon Worcestershire sauce
 1 dash Tabasco
 ½ cup thinly sliced scallions
 3 large egg whites

Preheat oven to 375° F. Spread butter onto side of a 5-cup soufflé dish and coat with bread crumbs.

In a heavy saucepan stir together tomato paste and 1 tablespoon milk. Sprinkle half of flour over tomato mixture and stir until smooth. Stir in 1 tablespoon milk and sprinkle with remaining flour, stirring until smooth. Stir in remaining 6 tablespoons milk and cook over moderately low heat, stirring constantly, 3 minutes (mixture will be very thick). Add Gorgonzola and garlic and cook, stirring, until cheese is melted. Stir in Worcestershire sauce, Tabasco, scallions, and salt to taste and keep warm, covered.

Working quickly, in another bowl with a whisk or an electric mixer beat egg whites with a pinch salt until they just hold stiff peaks. Stir about one fourth of whites into cheese mixture to lighten and fold in remaining whites gently but thoroughly. Turn mixture into soufflé dish and bake in middle of oven until golden and puffed, about 20 minutes. Serve soufflé immediately. Serves 2.

Each serving: 121 calories, 3 grams fat (22% of calories from fat)

CHEDDAR GRITS WITH FRIED TOMATOES

 2¼ cups water
 ½ teaspoon salt
 ⅓ cup white hominy grits (not quick-cooking)
 ½ cup plus 3 tablespoons grated sharp Cheddar
 ¼ teaspoon Tabasco
 2 tablespoons unsalted butter
 2 firm vine-ripened tomatoes (about 1 pound), sliced ¼ inch thick

Butter an 8- or 9-inch cake pan.

In a heavy saucepan bring water with salt to a boil and add grits in a slow stream, whisking. Simmer grits, covered, stirring frequently, until thickened, about 15 minutes. Stir in ½ cup Cheddar and Tabasco and spread grits in cake pan.

Preheat broiler.

In a heavy skillet heat butter over moderately high heat until foam subsides and fry tomatoes about 30 seconds on each side, or until golden but not falling apart. Arrange tomatoes on top of grits, overlapping if necessary, and sprinkle evenly with remaining 3 tablespoons Cheddar. Broil casserole set about 6 inches from heat until cheese is bubbling. Serves 2 as a side dish.

LEEK AND GRUYÈRE QUICHE

For pastry shell

⅓ cup plus 3 tablespoons
all-purpose flour

3 tablespoons cold unsalted butter

1 tablespoon cold vegetable
shortening

1½ tablespoons ice water plus
additional if necessary

For filling

2 tablespoons unsalted butter

2 cups thinly sliced white and pale
green parts of leeks, washed well
and drained

1 small garlic clove, minced

¼ teaspoon dried thyme, crumbled

2 large eggs

⅓ cup heavy cream or milk

¼ cup coarsely grated Gruyère cheese

Preheat oven to 425° F.

Make pastry shell:

In a bowl with a pastry blender or in a small food processor blend or pulse together flour, 3 tablespoons butter, shortening, and a pinch salt until mixture resembles coarse meal. Add 1½ tablespoons ice water and toss with a fork or pulse until water is incorporated. Add enough additional ice water, 1 teaspoon at a time, tossing or pulsing to incorporate, until mixture begins to form a dough. Pat dough onto bottom and ½ inch up side of a 7½-inch tart pan with a removable fluted rim or a 9-inch pie plate and bake in lower third of oven until set and pale golden, about 7 minutes.

Make filling while shell is baking:

In a large skillet heat 2 tablespoons butter over moderately high heat until foam subsides and sauté leeks, stirring, 4 minutes,

or until wilted and tender. Remove skillet from heat and stir in garlic, thyme, and salt and pepper to taste. In a small bowl whisk together eggs and cream or milk. Sprinkle Gruyère over bottom of shell and spread leeks over it. Pour egg mixture over leeks.

Bake quiche on a baking sheet in middle of oven 15 minutes. Reduce oven temperature to 350° F. and bake quiche until set, about 8 minutes more. Serves 2.

ONION AND BLACK PEPPER FLATBREAD

Fast-acting yeast—found under the brand names RapidRise and Quick-Rise, and available in most supermarkets—is a stronger strain of yeast which causes dough to rise fifty percent faster than active dry yeast. It never needs proofing.

1¼ cups chopped onion

3 tablespoons plus 1 teaspoon
olive oil

2¼ cups all-purpose flour plus
additional if necessary

2½ teaspoons fast-acting yeast
(a ¼-ounce package)

¾ cup hot water (125 to 130° F.)

¾ teaspoon table salt

¾ teaspoon coarsely ground black
pepper plus additional for
sprinkling dough

½ teaspoon coarse salt

Preheat oven to 500° F. and lightly oil a large baking sheet.

In a small skillet cook 1 cup onion in 1 tablespoon oil over moderate heat, stirring occasionally, until golden brown. In a food processor combine 1 cup flour and yeast.

In a cup combine hot water and 1 tablespoon oil. With motor running add hot water mixture and turn motor off. Add 1¼ cups flour, table salt, and ¾ teaspoon pepper and pulse 4 times. Add cooked onion and blend, pulsing in additional flour, 1 tablespoon at a time, if necessary to keep dough from sticking, until dough forms a ball. Transfer dough to a lightly floured surface and knead 15 seconds.

Quarter dough and form each piece into a ¼-inch-thick round. Arrange rounds on baking sheet and, with a finger, press indentations firmly into dough every 2 inches. Drizzle dough with remaining 4 teaspoons oil and sprinkle with remaining ¼ cup onion, additional pepper, and coarse salt. Bake bread in middle of oven 15 minutes, or until golden. Makes four 5-inch flatbreads.

Photo on page 93

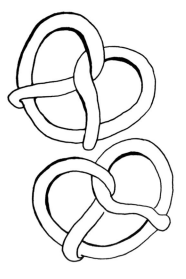

PARMESAN SCALLION PRETZELS

1½ cups all-purpose flour
½ teaspoon fast-acting yeast
⅓ cup hot water (125 to 130° F.)
½ teaspoon olive oil
1 large egg, lightly beaten with
   1 tablespoon water
3 tablespoons freshly grated
   Parmesan
¼ cup thinly sliced scallion greens
   coarse salt to taste

Preheat oven to 400° F. and butter 2 baking sheets.

In a food processor blend ½ cup flour and yeast. With motor running add hot water and turn motor off. Add ½ cup flour, oil, 1 teaspoon egg mixture, Parmesan, and scallions and blend until mixture just forms a ball. Let dough rise in processor bowl in a warm place 15 minutes.

On a floured surface knead in enough of remaining ½ cup flour to form a smooth and elastic dough. Roll out dough into a 12- by 4-inch rectangle and with a pizza cutter or sharp knife cut lengthwise into 16 strips. Roll strips gently to form ropes and on baking sheets form ropes into pretzel shapes. Brush pretzels with some remaining egg mixture and sprinkle generously with coarse salt. Bake pretzels in oven 12 minutes, or until golden. Transfer pretzels to a rack and cool. Makes 16 pretzels.

PASTA AND GRAINS

Pasta

ARTICHOKE AND OLIVE MARINARA SAUCE

Here's a robust marinara sauce filled with Mediterranean flavors that cooks in 20 minutes. Pair it with any substantial pasta, such as penne, that will hold the sauce.

> 2 garlic cloves, minced
> ¾ cup finely chopped onion
> 1½ tablespoons minced drained bottled *peperoncini* (pickled Tuscan peppers)
> ¼ cup olive oil
> ⅓ cup dry white wine
> 1 28-ounce can whole tomatoes including juice, chopped
> 2 6-ounce jars marinated artichoke hearts, drained well and halved lengthwise
> ½ cup chopped pitted Kalamata olives
> ⅓ cup minced fresh parsley leaves

In a large skillet cook garlic, onion, and *peperoncini* in oil over moderately low heat, stirring, until onion is softened. Add wine and boil 3 minutes, or until most of wine is evaporated. Add tomatoes with juice and simmer, stirring occasionally, 20 minutes, or until thickened. Stir artichoke hearts and olives into sauce and simmer 5 minutes. Stir in parsley and salt and pepper to taste. Makes about 4 cups, enough for 1 pound dried pasta, cooked, such as *penne*. May be doubled.

Photo opposite

ROSEMARY LEMON COUSCOUS

Couscous, although it has a grainlike texture, is actually a pasta made from finely ground semolina.

> ¾ cup chicken broth
> 2 teaspoons extra-virgin olive oil
> 1½ teaspoons fresh lemon juice, or to taste
> ½ teaspoon finely chopped fresh rosemary leaves or a pinch dried rosemary, crumbled
> ¼ teaspoon salt
> ½ cup couscous
> 2 teaspoons minced fresh parsley leaves

In a small saucepan stir together broth, oil, lemon juice, rosemary, and salt and bring to a boil, covered. Stir in couscous and remove pan from heat. Let mixture stand, covered, 5 minutes. Fluff couscous with a fork and stir in parsley and pepper to taste. Serves 2 as a side dish. May be doubled.

Artichoke and Olive Marinara Sauce

COUSCOUS WITH TOMATO AND SMOKED SAUSAGE

¼ cup finely chopped pork and beef smoked hot sausage link (about 1 ounce)
¼ cup finely chopped onion
1 garlic clove, minced
½ cup canned whole tomatoes, drained and chopped fine
¾ cup water
½ cup couscous
2 tablespoons finely chopped scallion greens

In a 1½- to 2-quart heavy saucepan cook sausage and onion over moderate heat, stirring occasionally, until sausage is lightly browned. Add garlic and cook, stirring, until fragrant, about 15 seconds. Stir in tomatoes and water and bring to a boil. Stir in couscous and remove pan from heat. Let mixture stand, covered, 5 minutes. Fluff couscous with a fork and stir in scallion greens and salt to taste. Serves 2 as a side dish. May be doubled.

Each serving: 265 calories, 5 grams fat (17% of calories from fat)

PASTA WITH UNCOOKED TOMATO AND OLIVE SAUCE

Fresh ingredients are key to our uncooked tomato sauce, so enjoy this recipe when your greenmarket is filled with lush summer tomatoes and herbs. To quickly peel garlic, lightly crush cloves with the flat side of a large heavy knife. The skins will fall away easily.

3 medium vine-ripened tomatoes, seeded and chopped
1 medium yellow bell pepper, chopped fine
2 garlic cloves, or to taste, minced
1 cup coarsely grated mozzarella (about 4 ounces)
½ cup Niçoise or other brine-cured black olives, pitted and halved
3 tablespoons extra-virgin olive oil
1 tablespoon balsamic vinegar, or to taste
½ pound *cavatappi* (sometimes called *tortiglioni* or *serpentini*) or other spiral-shaped pasta such as *rotini*
¾ cup finely chopped mixed fresh herbs such as basil, parsley, and mint leaves

In a large bowl stir together tomatoes, bell pepper, garlic, mozzarella, olives, oil, vinegar, and salt and pepper to taste and let stand 30 minutes.

While sauce is standing, in a 3½-quart kettle bring 2 quarts salted water to a boil. Add pasta and cook until *al dente*.

Drain pasta well in a colander and add to sauce. Add herbs and toss well. Serves 2. May be doubled.

Photo opposite

Pasta with Uncooked Tomato and Olive Sauce

BAKED MACARONI AND RATATOUILLE

1   small onion, chopped
1   garlic clove, minced
1½ tablespoons olive oil
1½ cups finely chopped eggplant
    (about ¼ pound)
⅓ cup finely chopped zucchini
⅓ cup finely chopped red bell pepper
½ cup canned whole tomatoes with
    juice, tomatoes chopped
½ teaspoon dried basil, crumbled
¼ teaspoon dried thyme, crumbled
½ cup elbow macaroni (about
    2 ounces)
2   tablespoons freshly grated
    Parmesan

In a large skillet cook onion and garlic in oil over moderately low heat, stirring, until onion is softened. Add eggplant, zucchini, and bell pepper and sauté over moderately high heat, stirring, until softened. Stir in tomatoes with juice, basil, thyme, and salt and pepper to taste and simmer *ratatouille*, stirring occasionally, 20 minutes.

Preheat oven to 400° F.

While *ratatouille* is simmering, bring a large saucepan of salted water to a boil. Add macaroni and cook until *al dente*, about 12 minutes. Drain macaroni well in a colander.

Stir macaroni into *ratatouille* and transfer to an 8-inch square baking dish. Sprinkle top with Parmesan and bake in middle of oven until bubbling, about 10 minutes. Serves 2. May be doubled.

ORZO WITH MUSHROOMS, WALNUTS, AND SAGE

Here's an elegant side dish that combines exciting flavors and textures. Use your favorite exotic mushrooms, such as creminis, shiitakes, chanterelles, oyster mushrooms, or portobellos, or try a combination of two or three kinds. To clean mushrooms, cut off the sandy stems and brush off dirt from caps with either a small brush or a dampened paper towel.

- ¾ cup *orzo* (rice-shaped pasta)
- ½ cup chopped onion
- 1 garlic clove, minced
- 1½ tablespoons unsalted butter
- 8 ounces fresh mushrooms (preferably exotic), chopped
- ½ teaspoon dried sage, or to taste, crumbled
- 2 tablespoons dry red or white wine
- 2 tablespoons chopped walnuts, lightly toasted

Bring a 3½-quart saucepan filled with 2 quarts salted water to a boil. Add *orzo* and cook, stirring occasionally, until *al dente*, about 8 minutes. Drain *orzo* in a colander.

In a heavy saucepan cook onion and garlic in butter over moderate heat, stirring, until lightly browned and stir in mushrooms and sage. Cook mixture, stirring, until most of liquid mushrooms give off is evaporated. Stir in wine and cook 2 minutes. Stir in *orzo* and salt and pepper to taste.

Serve *orzo* sprinkled with walnuts. Serves 2 as a side dish. May be doubled.

ASIAN-STYLE NOODLES WITH CARROT AND SCALLION

- 2 ounces *spaghettini*
- 1½ tablespoons soy sauce
- 2 teaspoons white-wine vinegar
- 2 teaspoons Scotch
- 1 teaspoon vegetable oil
- 1 teaspoon grated peeled fresh gingerroot
- 1 garlic clove, minced and mashed to a paste with ¼ teaspoon salt
- 1½ teaspoons sugar
- ½ cup coarsely shredded carrot
- 3 tablespoons finely chopped scallion

Bring a large saucepan of salted water to a boil. Add *spaghettini* and cook until just tender, about 10 minutes. Drain *spaghettini* well in a colander.

While *spaghettini* is cooking, in a small heavy saucepan bring soy sauce, vinegar, Scotch, oil, gingerroot, garlic paste, and sugar to a boil, stirring until sugar is dissolved. Add carrot and simmer until crisp-tender, about 3 minutes.

Transfer carrot and sauce to a large bowl. Add pasta, scallion, and pepper to taste and toss to combine well. Serves 2 as a side dish. May be doubled.

Each serving: 172 calories, 3 grams fat (16% of calories from fat)

TAGLIATELLE WITH SMOKED SALMON AND CAPER SAUCE

½ pound *tagliatelle* or other long flat
  ribbon pasta such as fettuccine
½ cup chopped onion
½ cup chopped celery
2 tablespoons unsalted butter
1½ tablespoons drained capers,
  chopped fine
1 tablespoon minced fresh dill
3 ounces cream cheese, cut into pieces
3 ounces smoked salmon,
  chopped coarse

Bring a 3½-quart saucepan filled with 2 quarts salted water to a boil for pasta.

In a small skillet cook onion and celery in butter over moderately low heat, stirring, until tender. Stir in capers, dill, and salt and pepper to taste.

Add *tagliatelle* to boiling water and cook until *al dente*, about 8 minutes. Reserve ⅓ cup pasta cooking water in a large heated bowl and drain *tagliatelle* well in a colander. Whisk cream cheese into reserved cooking water until cheese is melted and mixture is smooth. Add *tagliatelle,* salmon, and caper mixture and toss well. Serves 2. May be doubled.

PEPPERONI SPAGHETTI CAKES

¼ pound spaghetti
⅓ cup finely chopped sliced pepperoni
⅓ cup finely chopped red bell pepper
¼ cup freshly grated Parmesan
½ cup thinly sliced scallion greens
2 garlic cloves, minced
1 large egg, lightly beaten
1 teaspoon vegetable oil

Garnish: two 3-inch pieces of scallion green

Accompaniment: sour cream

Bring a large saucepan of salted water to a boil. Add spaghetti and cook until *al dente*, about 12 minutes. While spaghetti is cooking, in a bowl toss together pepperoni, bell pepper, Parmesan, sliced scallion greens, garlic, and salt and pepper to taste. Drain spaghetti well in a colander and add to pepperoni mixture, tossing well. Add egg and toss until combined well.

In a 6-inch non-stick skillet heat ½ teaspoon oil over moderate heat until hot but not smoking and add half of spaghetti mixture, pressing it evenly into bottom of skillet. Cook spaghetti cake 3 minutes, or until underside is golden, and turn over. Cook spaghetti cake 3 minutes more, or until underside is golden, and transfer to a heated plate. Make another spaghetti cake in same manner with remaining ½ teaspoon oil and remaining spaghetti mixture and transfer to another heated plate.

Keeping ½ inch of one end of each scallion piece intact, make lengthwise cuts to form brushes. Spoon a dollop of sour cream onto each spaghetti cake and garnish with scallion brushes. Serves 2. May be doubled.

Photo opposite

GORGONZOLA RAVIOLI WITH ROASTED PEPPER PESTO

Won ton wrappers, found in Asian markets and most supermarkets, make a quick fresh pasta substitute in this recipe. Like any stuffed fresh pasta, won ton ravioli are fragile, so be sure to cook them in gently boiling water, then carefully scoop them from the water with a slotted spoon onto paper towels to drain.

For filling

- ½ cup chopped onion
- 3 tablespoons pine nuts
- 1 tablespoon olive oil
- ½ cup crumbled Gorgonzola cheese (about 2 ounces)

- 16 won ton wrappers, thawed if frozen

For pesto

- ½ cup firmly packed fresh parsley leaves
- 1 tablespoon pine nuts
- 1 small garlic clove
- 2½ tablespoons chopped bottled roasted red pepper
- 2 tablespoons olive oil
- 1 teaspoon fresh lemon juice

Make filling:

In a small skillet cook onion and pine nuts in oil over moderate heat, stirring occasionally, until golden. In a bowl with a fork mash together onion mixture, Gorgonzola, and pepper to taste.

Bring a 3½-quart saucepan of salted water to a gentle boil for won tons.

Arrange 1 won ton wrapper on a lightly floured surface and moisten edge. Mound about 1 tablespoon filling in center. Arrange another wrapper over filling and pinch edges together, pressing out any air bubbles and sealing edges well. Transfer ravioli to a kitchen towel. Make more ravioli with remaining wrappers and filling in same manner, turning ravioli occasionally to dry slightly.

Add ravioli to gently boiling water and cook 6 minutes, or until they rise to surface and are tender. (Do not let water boil vigorously once ravioli have been added.) With a slotted spoon transfer ravioli as cooked to a kitchen towel to drain.

Make pesto while ravioli are cooking:

In a blender or small food processor purée pesto ingredients and season with salt and pepper.

Divide ravioli between 2 plates and spoon pesto over them. Serves 2. May be doubled.

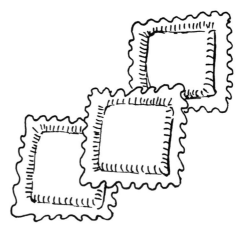

Grains

BULGUR PILAF WITH CURRANTS, CUMIN, AND MINT

Bulgur, a wheat grain popular in the Middle East, is available at natural foods stores, specialty foods shops, and most supermarkets. Our pilaf combines the nutlike taste of bulgur with the flavors of scallions, currants, and mint for an aromatic side dish.

¼ cup sliced scallions
½ teaspoon ground cumin
1 tablespoon vegetable oil
½ cup bulgur
¾ cup water
¼ cup dried currants
½ teaspoon salt
1 tablespoon packed fresh mint
  leaves, chopped fine

In a small heavy saucepan cook scallions and cumin in oil over moderately low heat, stirring, until softened. Add bulgur and cook, stirring, 1 minute. Add water, currants, and salt and bring liquid to a boil. Cook mixture, covered, over low heat 10 minutes, or until liquid is absorbed, and stir in mint. Remove pan from heat and let pilaf stand, covered, 5 minutes. Serves 2. May be doubled.

CURRIED RICE WITH CARAMELIZED ONION

¾ cup thinly sliced onion
1 tablespoon vegetable oil
½ cup converted rice
1 teaspoon curry powder
1 cup water
½ teaspoon salt
2 teaspoons finely chopped fresh
  coriander sprigs

In a heavy saucepan cook onion in oil over moderate heat, stirring, until golden brown. Add rice and curry powder and cook mixture, stirring, 2 minutes. Add water and salt and boil over high heat until water is reduced to just below level of rice. Reduce heat to very low and cook, covered, 15 minutes, or until liquid is absorbed and rice is tender. Fluff rice with a fork and stir in coriander. Serves 2. May be doubled.

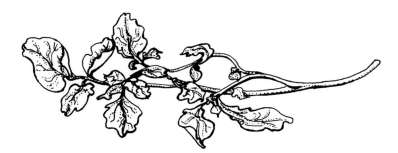

RICE SALAD WITH WATERCRESS

Rice salads served at room temperature make ideal al fresco side dishes. Here, a tiny bit of olive oil and a tablespoon of vinegar are all that is needed to dress the rice, resulting in a low-fat dish. Flat-leafed parsley can be substituted for the watercress if desired.

½ cup long-grain white rice
¼ teaspoon ground cumin
½ teaspoon salt
1 cup water
1 tablespoon white-wine vinegar
2 teaspoons olive oil
1 cup chopped watercress leaves with tender stems
2 tablespoons finely chopped scallion

In a 1½- to 2-quart heavy saucepan bring rice, cumin, salt, and water to a boil and cook, covered, over low heat until water is absorbed and rice is tender, about 17 minutes. Fluff rice with a fork and transfer to a bowl. Sprinkle rice with vinegar and oil and toss to combine well. Cool rice mixture, tossing occasionally, 10 minutes. Add watercress, scallion, and salt and pepper to taste and toss to combine well. Serves 2. May be doubled.

Each serving: 214 calories, 5 grams fat (21% of calories from fat)

FRIED RICE WITH SPINACH

⅓ cup long-grain white rice
⅔ cup chicken broth
½ 10-ounce package frozen chopped spinach
1½ tablespoons vegetable oil
1½ teaspoons minced peeled fresh gingerroot
2 scallions, sliced thin
1 tablespoon soy sauce
2 teaspoons white-wine vinegar or distilled white vinegar

In a bowl wash rice well in several changes of cold water, draining it in a sieve. In a small heavy saucepan bring broth to a boil. Add rice and cook, covered, over low heat 17 minutes, or until water is absorbed.

While rice is cooking, cook spinach according to package instructions and drain well. Cool spinach completely and squeeze dry by handfuls.

Fluff rice with a fork and transfer to a bowl. Let rice cool 10 minutes.

In a wok or heavy skillet heat oil over high heat until hot but not smoking and stir-fry gingerroot until fragrant, about 5 seconds. Add rice, spinach, and scallions and stir-fry 1 minute. Add soy sauce and vinegar and stir-fry 30 seconds. Season fried rice with salt and pepper. Serves 2. May be doubled.

RISOTTO WITH SWISS CHARD

Risotto, traditionally made with Arborio rice (Italian short-grain rice), gradually releases starch and expands as it cooks in broth. Long-grain rice, however, may be used with excellent results. Add broth to the rice mixture, a small ladleful at a time, stirring constantly, and wait for the rice to absorb the broth before adding more.

½ pound Swiss chard (preferably red), washed well and drained
1 garlic clove, minced
1¾ cups chicken broth
1¼ cups water
½ cup long-grain white rice
¼ teaspoon freshly grated lemon zest
2 tablespoons freshly grated Parmesan

Tear Swiss chard leaves from stems and coarsely chop leaves. Trim stems and finely chop enough stems to measure ½ cup, reserving remainder for another use.

In a 3-quart heavy saucepan simmer chard stems and garlic in ½ cup broth, covered, until tender, about 5 minutes. In another saucepan bring water and remaining 1¼ cups broth to a simmer and keep at a bare simmer.

Stir rice and zest into chard-stem mixture and cook, stirring, 1 minute. Stir in ¼ cup broth and cook, stirring constantly and keeping at a simmer, until broth is absorbed. Continue simmering and adding broth, about ¼ cup at a time, stirring constantly and letting each addition be absorbed before adding next, until about half of broth has been added. Stir in chard leaves and continue simmering and adding broth in same manner until rice is tender and creamy-looking but still *al dente*, about 18 minutes. Stir in Parmesan and salt and pepper to taste. Serves 2 as an entrée. May be doubled.

Each serving: 291 calories, 5 grams fat (15% of calories from fat)

VEGETABLE STEW WITH COUSCOUS

For the greens in this stew choose either mustard greens with a peppery and slightly bitter bite, or Swiss chard with milder flavor.

- 1 tablespoon olive oil
- 1 small butternut squash (about 1½ pounds), peeled, seeded, and cut into 2-inch pieces
- 1 medium onion, cut into 6 wedges
- 1 cup water
- ⅔ cup couscous
- 2 teaspoons minced fresh parsley leaves
- ½ pound mushrooms, halved
- 1 cup low-salt chicken or vegetable broth
- ¼ cup apple cider or juice
- 2 teaspoons all-purpose flour
- ¼ cup raisins
- ¼ pound mustard greens or Swiss chard, stems and center ribs discarded and greens washed, spun dry, and coarsely chopped (about 2 cups)

In a large non-stick skillet heat oil over moderately high heat until hot but not smoking and sauté squash and onion with salt to taste, stirring occasionally, until lightly browned, about 5 minutes. Reduce heat to moderately low and cook, covered, stirring occasionally, about 5 minutes, or until squash is almost tender.

While squash mixture is cooking, in a small saucepan bring water to a boil. Stir in couscous and let stand, covered, off heat 5 minutes. Stir in parsley and salt to taste and keep warm, covered.

Add mushrooms to squash mixture and sauté over moderately high heat, stirring occasionally, until mushrooms are golden. In a large measuring cup stir together broth, cider or juice, and flour until smooth. Stir broth mixture and raisins into vegetable mixture and simmer over moderate heat until sauce is slightly thickened, about 2 minutes. Put greens or chard on top of stew and season with salt. Simmer stew, covered, 1 minute, or until greens are wilted.

Serve stew with couscous. Serves 2 as an entrée. May be doubled.

Photo opposite

Vegetable Stew with Couscous

SESAME ASPARAGUS

    1 pound asparagus, trimmed and cut
       diagonally into 1½-inch pieces
    ½ cup finely chopped scallions
    2 teaspoons soy sauce
    1 teaspoon sesame seeds, toasted
    ½ teaspoon Asian sesame oil

Arrange asparagus, with tips on top, in a
steamer rack set in a saucepan of boiling
water. Steam asparagus, covered, until crisp-
tender, about 4 minutes. In a bowl stir
together remaining ingredients and pepper
to taste and add asparagus, tossing to coat.
Serves 2. May be doubled.

Each serving: 81 calories, 3 grams fat
(33% of calories from fat)

SPICY SAUTÉED GREEN BEANS WITH BACON

*Fresh long green beans or thin haricots verts are
equally delicious in our recipe. To trim green
beans, snap off the stem end, pulling it toward the
tail end to remove any string. For tougher beans,
repeat with the tail end.*

    3 slices bacon, chopped
    6 ounces green beans, trimmed and
       cut into 1½-inch pieces
    ¼ cup water
    1 small garlic clove, minced
    ¼ teaspoon dried hot red pepper
       flakes
    ¼ cup thinly sliced scallions

In a large skillet or wok cook bacon over
moderate heat, stirring occasionally, until

crisp and transfer with a slotted spoon to a
bowl. Heat fat remaining in skillet or wok
over moderately high heat until hot but not
smoking and sauté beans 2 minutes. Stir in
water, garlic, and red pepper flakes and
simmer, covered, until beans are tender, 5
to 8 minutes. Stir in scallions and bacon.
Serves 2. May be doubled.

LIMA BEAN PURÉE WITH OLIVE OIL AND OREGANO

*For an even faster purée, blend the lima bean
mixture right in the pan with a hand-held mixer.
The purée will be slightly chunkier.*

    a 10-ounce package frozen lima beans
       (unthawed)
    ¼ cup water
    2 teaspoons extra-virgin olive oil
    ½ teaspoon white-wine vinegar
    ¼ teaspoon dried oregano, crumbled
    a pinch sugar

Accompaniment: toasted garlic bread

In a small saucepan bring lima beans and
water to a boil and simmer, covered, stirring occasionally to break up beans, about 8
minutes and transfer beans with liquid to a
food processor. Add remaining ingredients
and salt and pepper to taste and purée until
smooth.

Serve purée as a spread on garlic toast or
as a side dish. Serves 2. May be doubled.

Photo on page 84

BRUSSELS SPROUTS AND ONIONS WITH DILL

To peel onions quickly, cut a small "x" in each (not on root end) and boil for 1 minute, or until skins slip off easily; then quarter.

1½ tablespoons vegetable oil
6 small white onions (each about 1 inch in diameter), peeled and quartered
12 Brussels sprouts, trimmed and quartered
¼ cup water
1 teaspoon sugar
1 teaspoon minced fresh dill

Garnish: fresh dill sprigs

In a 10-inch heavy skillet heat oil over moderately high heat until hot but not smoking and sauté onions and Brussels sprouts, stirring, until onions begin to turn golden, about 1½ minutes. Add water, sugar, and salt and pepper to taste and cook, covered, over moderately low heat until vegetables are just tender and nearly all liquid is evaporated, about 3 minutes. Stir in minced dill.

Garnish vegetables with dill sprigs. Serves 2. May be doubled.

Photo on page 100

STEAMED CAULIFLOWER WITH CARAWAY BUTTERMILK SAUCE

For a change of pace, look for the new cauliflower varieties: purple cauliflower has the same taste as white, but is slightly less crisp; bright yellow-green broccoflower, a cross between cauliflower and broccoli, is a little milder tasting than white.

3 cups 1-inch cauliflower flowerets
½ cup buttermilk
1 teaspoon all-purpose flour
1 tablespoon packed grated extra-sharp Cheddar
¼ teaspoon caraway seeds, lightly toasted

Arrange cauliflower in a steamer rack set in a saucepan of boiling water and steam, covered, until just tender, about 5 minutes. While cauliflower is steaming, in a cup stir together 1 tablespoon buttermilk and flour until smooth. In a small heavy saucepan cook Cheddar and remaining 7 tablespoons buttermilk over moderate heat, stirring, until cheese is melted. Whisk in flour paste and simmer, whisking, 4 minutes, or until sauce is slightly thickened. Stir in caraway seeds and salt and pepper to taste. In a bowl toss cauliflower with sauce. Serves 2. May be doubled.

Each serving: 88 calories, 2 grams fat (20% of calories from fat)

BLACK BEAN TOSTADAS WITH CURLY ENDIVE SALAD

If you prefer to crisp tortillas without frying them, heat a dry heavy skillet, preferably cast-iron, over moderate heat until it is just smoking and cook tortillas one at a time, turning them frequently with tongs, until the tortillas are hot and crisp, about 3 minutes.

¾ teaspoon ground cumin
1 tablespoon wine vinegar, or to taste
3 tablespoons olive oil
1 avocado (preferably California)
1 15- to 16-ounce can black beans, rinsed and drained
¼ cup chopped drained sun-dried tomatoes packed in oil
1 scallion, chopped
vegetable oil for frying
2 6- to 7-inch corn tortillas
3 cups torn inner leaves of curly endive (chicory), washed and spun dry
⅓ cup thinly sliced red cabbage

In a bowl whisk together cumin, vinegar, and salt to taste and whisk in olive oil until combined well. Halve avocado and discard pit. Peel avocado and cut into 1-inch pieces. In a bowl toss avocado gently with beans, tomatoes, scallion, two-thirds dressing, and salt and pepper to taste.

In a heavy skillet heat ½ inch vegetable oil over moderate heat until hot but not smoking and fry tortillas, 1 at a time, turning with tongs, until pale golden and crisp, about 1½ minutes. Transfer tortillas with tongs to paper towels to drain. In another bowl toss endive and cabbage with remaining dressing and salt and pepper to taste.

Arrange tortillas on 2 plates and top with black bean mixture and endive salad. Serves 2. May be doubled.

Photo opposite

STEAMED ACORN SQUASH WITH MOLASSES

Acorn squash is pleasant and creamy-tasting— the dark green variety, sometimes streaked with orange, is the most flavorful and the least fibrous; the orange variety tends to be blander.

1 small acorn squash (about 1 pound)
1 tablespoon unsulfured molasses
2 teaspoons fresh lemon juice

Quarter squash lengthwise and discard seeds and membranes. Arrange squash, flesh side down, on a steamer rack set in a saucepan of boiling water and steam, covered, until tender, about 12 minutes. In a small bowl stir together molasses and lemon juice. Transfer squash with tongs to a plate and season with salt. Drizzle squash with molasses mixture. Serves 2. May be doubled.

Each serving: 151 calories, 0 grams fat (0% of calories from fat)

PARSNIPS AND PEAS WITH HONEY MUSTARD GLAZE

Most parsnip recipes call for slow gentle cooking of this carrot cousin. We've speeded things up here by cutting the parsnips into dice, and boiling, then sautéing them in the same pan, to bring out their sweet and nutty flavor.

    2 teaspoons honey
    2 teaspoons Dijon mustard
    6 tablespoons water
    ½ pound parsnips, peeled and cut
       into ½-inch cubes
    1 tablespoon olive oil
    ¾ cup frozen peas (unthawed)
    1 tablespoon minced fresh parsley
       leaves

In a bowl stir together honey, mustard, and 2 tablespoons water.

In a 10-inch non-stick skillet boil parsnips, remaining ¼ cup water, and oil, covered, until water is evaporated. Remove lid and cook parsnips over moderate heat, stirring occasionally, until golden and tender, about 5 minutes.

While parsnips are boiling, bring a saucepan of salted water to a boil and cook peas until tender, about 5 minutes. Drain peas and add to parsnips. Stir in honey mixture and simmer 1 minute. Stir in parsley and season with salt and pepper. Serves 2. May be doubled.

CREAMED FENNEL AND CARROTS

    2 large carrots, cut into ¼-inch-thick
       slices (about 1 cup)
    1 small fennel bulb (sometimes called
       anise), trimmed and sliced ¼-inch
       thick (about 1½ cups)
    ½ cup water
    3 tablespoons fresh orange juice
    ½ tablespoon unsalted butter
    ⅓ cup heavy cream

In a small heavy saucepan stir together all ingredients except cream and simmer, covered, 20 minutes. Remove lid and boil until water is evaporated and vegetables begin to brown, about 3 minutes. Stir in cream and salt and pepper to taste. Serves 2. May be doubled.

SAVORY MUSHROOMS IN WINE SAUCE

¼ cup finely chopped shallot
1 small garlic clove, finely chopped
2 tablespoons unsalted butter
½ pound small mushrooms, quartered
  (about 3 cups)
2 tablespoons dry red or white wine
3 tablespoons water
1 tablespoon Worcestershire sauce
2 teaspoons ketchup

In a skillet cook shallot and garlic in butter over moderately low heat, stirring, until softened. Add mushrooms and cook over moderate heat until they begin to give off liquid. Stir in wine and simmer 2 minutes. Stir in remaining ingredients and simmer 3 minutes. Serves 2. May be doubled.

GRUYÈRE POTATO GRATIN

The potatoes for our gratin are parboiled briefly before baking to speed up cooking and ensure that they will be tender. For quick cleanup, rinse the saucepan with cold water (don't dry) before heating the milk.

1 pound large red potatoes
¾ cup coarsely grated Gruyère cheese
  (about 3 ounces)
1 large egg
1 cup milk

Preheat oven to 400° F. and butter a 1½-quart gratin or other shallow baking dish.

Bring a large saucepan of salted water to a boil. Peel potatoes and cut into thin slices (about ⅛-inch thick). Add potatoes to boiling water and cook 4 minutes (potatoes will not be tender). Drain potatoes well in a colander.

In baking dish arrange potatoes, overlapping them, in 3 layers, sprinkling first 2 layers each with ¼ cup Gruyère and salt and pepper to taste.

In a small saucepan bring milk just to a boil. In a small bowl whisk egg and add hot milk in a stream, whisking. Season mixture with salt and pepper and pour over potatoes. Sprinkle potatoes with remaining ¼ cup cheese and bake 30 minutes, or until top is golden and potatoes are tender. Serves 2 generously.

Photo on page 109

SAUTÉED JERUSALEM ARTICHOKES WITH PEPPERS

Jerusalem artichokes are notoriously difficult to peel, especially if they are very knobby. To avoid peeling them, trim off protruding knobs, then scrub the skins thoroughly with a stiff brush to remove any traces of dirt.

½ pound Jerusalem artichokes (sometimes called sunchokes)
1½ tablespoons olive oil
½ red bell pepper, cut into ¾-inch pieces
½ *jalapeño* chili, seeded and minced (wear rubber gloves)
1 tablespoon minced shallot
1 tablespoon minced fresh coriander sprigs

Garnish: fresh coriander leaves

Peel artichokes and cut into ¼-inch-thick slices. In a heavy skillet heat oil over moderately high heat until hot but not smoking and sauté artichokes, stirring, 8 minutes, or until tender and lightly browned. Season artichokes with salt and with a slotted spoon transfer to a plate. Add bell pepper to skillet and cook over moderate heat, stirring, 1 minute. Add *jalapeño* and cook, stirring, 1 minute. Stir in shallot and cook, stirring, 1 minute, or until bell pepper is crisp-tender. Stir in artichokes and remove skillet from heat. Stir in minced coriander and salt and pepper to taste.

Serve vegetables garnished with coriander leaves. Serves 2. May be doubled.

Photo opposite

GARLIC YOGURT GRILLED OKRA

⅓ cup plain low-fat yogurt
1 garlic clove, minced and mashed to a paste with ¼ teaspoon salt
½ teaspoon ground cumin
1 pinch cayenne
½ pound small okra, rinsed and patted dry

In a bowl stir together yogurt, garlic paste, cumin, and cayenne and add okra, tossing until combined well. Marinate okra, covered, at room temperature 15 minutes.

Prepare grill.

Remove okra from marinade, letting excess drip off, and grill on an oiled rack set 5 to 6 inches over glowing coals until tender, about 6 minutes on each side. (Alternatively, okra may be broiled on rack of a broiler pan lined with foil about 4 inches from heat in same manner.) Brush okra with remaining marinade. Serves 2. May be doubled.

Each serving: 64 calories, 1 gram fat (14% of calories from fat)

SWEET POTATO PURÉE

1 pound sweet potatoes
2 tablespoons unsalted butter, cut into
   bits and softened
2 tablespoons sour cream
1 tablespoon firmly packed brown
   sugar

Peel sweet potatoes and halve lengthwise.
Cut halves crosswise into ¼-inch-thick
slices. In a saucepan simmer potatoes in
water to cover until tender, about 5 minutes,
and drain. Return potatoes to pan and cook
over moderate heat, shaking pan occasionally, until excess water is evaporated. In a
food processor purée potatoes with remaining ingredients until smooth and season
with salt. Serves 2. May be doubled.
   Photo on front jacket

ROASTED POTATOES WITH CORIANDER AND ONION

1 pound small red potatoes,
   quartered
3 tablespoons olive oil
1 small red onion, sliced thin
3 tablespoons fresh lemon juice
1 tablespoon water
½ teaspoon salt
1½ tablespoons finely chopped fresh
   coriander sprigs

Preheat oven to 425° F.
   In a baking pan toss together potatoes
and 2 tablespoons oil and roast in middle of
oven, stirring occasionally, until potatoes are
golden, about 25 minutes.
   While potatoes are roasting, in a skillet
cook onion in remaining tablespoon oil over
moderate heat, stirring, until softened, about
10 minutes. Stir in lemon juice, water, salt,
and pepper to taste and cook, stirring, until
almost all liquid is evaporated. Add potatoes
and coriander and toss until combined well.
Serves 2. May be doubled.

PROVENÇAL-STYLE SUMMER SQUASH AND TOMATO GRATIN

Summer squash is plentiful in the summer months—tender-skinned crookneck, straightneck, and pattypan or other scallop varieties may be substituted in our gratin with excellent results.

2 tablespoons olive oil
1 teaspoon minced garlic
1 zucchini, cut diagonally into ¼-inch-thick slices
1 yellow squash, cut diagonally into ¼-inch-thick slices
1 vine-ripened tomato, cut into ¼-inch-thick slices and slices halved
6 fresh basil leaves, chopped fine
2 tablespoons freshly grated Parmesan

Preheat oven to 425° F.

Coat bottom of a 1-quart gratin dish or 9-inch pie plate with 1 tablespoon oil and sprinkle evenly with garlic. Arrange zucchini, yellow squash, and tomato over garlic in one layer, alternating them and overlapping slightly. Drizzle vegetables with remaining tablespoon oil and sprinkle with basil, Parmesan, and salt and pepper to taste.

Bake gratin in middle of oven until golden, about 35 minutes. Serves 2 generously.

STIR-FRIED SPINACH WITH GINGER AND GARLIC

1 10-ounce bag fresh spinach or 2 small bunches (about 1¼ pounds total)
2 teaspoons vegetable oil
1 teaspoon minced peeled fresh gingerroot
1 garlic clove, minced

Wash spinach well, discarding coarse stems, and drain in a colander. In a wok or large heavy skillet heat oil over moderately high heat until hot but not smoking and stir-fry gingerroot and garlic until fragrant, 10 to 15 seconds. Add spinach with water clinging to its leaves and stir-fry until wilted, about 1 minute. Season spinach with salt and pepper. Serves 2. May be doubled.

Photo on page 109

BLACK BEAN AND ROASTED VEGETABLE SALAD

1 cup fresh corn (cut from 2 ears) or frozen corn (unthawed if frozen)
1 red bell pepper, cut into ½-inch-thick strips
1 onion, cut into ¼-inch-thick slices
2 teaspoons vegetable oil
3 tablespoons balsamic vinegar
1 16-ounce can black beans, rinsed and drained
2 tablespoons chopped fresh basil leaves

Preheat oven to 425° F.

In a large bowl toss corn, bell pepper, onion, oil, 1 tablespoon vinegar, and salt and pepper to taste to combine. In a shallow roasting pan spread vegetables evenly and roast in middle of oven until vegetables are tender, about 25 minutes. Cool vegetables slightly and in a bowl toss with beans, basil, remaining 2 tablespoons vinegar, and salt and pepper to taste. Serves 2. May be doubled.

Photo on front jacket

Each serving: 303 calories, 6 grams fat (18% of calories from fat)

GRAPEFRUIT, BEET, AND BLUE CHEESE SALAD

1 grapefruit
2 peeled cooked beets, coarsely grated (about 1 cup)
4 teaspoons extra-virgin olive oil
1 tablespoon balsamic vinegar
½ bunch watercress, washed well and spun dry, for lining plates
1 ounce chilled blue cheese, cut into small thin slices
coarse salt to taste
coarsely ground black pepper to taste

With a sharp knife cut peel and pith from grapefruit and working over a small bowl cut grapefruit sections free from membranes, letting sections drop into bowl. In another small bowl toss together beets, 2 teaspoons oil, and vinegar.

Line 2 plates with watercress. Arrange grapefruit sections and cheese decoratively on watercress and mound beets in center. Drizzle salads with remaining 2 teaspoons oil and sprinkle with salt and pepper. Serves 2. May be doubled.

Photo opposite

Grapefruit, Beet, and Blue Cheese Salad

Avocado and Hearts of Palm Salad with Ginger Lime Dressing

Hearts of palm are a delicacy that come from the inner portion of the palmetto (palm) tree. In Florida they sometimes can be found fresh; otherwise, they are sold canned, packed in water, at most supermarkets. Their mild flavor resembles artichoke.

1 tablespoon fresh lime juice
¼ teaspoon minced peeled fresh
  gingerroot
¼ teaspoon sugar
⅛ teaspoon cayenne
2 tablespoons vegetable oil
  Bibb lettuce leaves for lining plates
1 ripe avocado (preferably California)
½ 14-ounce can hearts of palm,
  drained and cut into ¼-inch-thick
  slices
1 teaspoon sesame seeds, lightly
  toasted

In a bowl whisk together lime juice, gingerroot, sugar, cayenne, and salt to taste. Add oil in a stream, whisking until dressing is combined well. Line 2 plates with lettuce. Halve avocado and discard pit. Peel avocado and cut into ¼-inch-thick slices. Arrange avocado slices, overlapping, on lettuce and top with hearts of palm. Drizzle salad with dressing and sprinkle with sesame seeds. Serves 2. May be doubled.

Avocado and Lime Caesar Salad with Chili Croutons

¼ loaf Italian bread, cut into ¾-inch
  cubes (about 1 cup)
3 tablespoons olive oil
½ teaspoon chili powder
1 small clove garlic, minced
  and mashed to a paste with
  ¼ teaspoon salt
2 flat anchovy fillets, minced
2 tablespoons mayonnaise
1½ tablespoons fresh lime juice, or to
  taste
½ teaspoon Worchestershire sauce
½ ripe avocado (preferably California)
1 head romaine, rinsed, spun dry,
  and torn into bite-size pieces
  (about 5 cups)
¼ cup freshly grated Parmesan

Preheat oven to 350° F.

In a bowl toss bread cubes with 1 tablespoon oil, chili powder, and salt to taste and on a baking sheet arrange in one layer. Bake cubes in middle of oven 10 minutes, or until golden, and cool. In a small bowl, stir together well garlic paste, anchovy, mayonnaise, lime juice, and Worcestershire sauce until smooth and whisk in remaining 2 tablespoons oil and salt and pepper to taste until combined well. Cut avocado into 1-inch pieces and in a bowl toss with romaine and dressing. Add Parmesan and croutons and toss until combined well. Serves 2 generously. May be doubled.

ARUGULA AND CARROT SALAD WITH WALNUT GRENADINE DRESSING

Grenadine, a sweet, nonalcoholic syrup made from pomegranate juice and a variety of herbs, is generally used in cocktails—here, it sweetens and colors our dressing.

- 2 tablespoons olive oil
- 1½ tablespoons white-wine vinegar
- 1½ tablespoons chopped walnuts
- 1½ teaspoons grenadine or maple syrup
- 2 cups loosely packed arugula leaves or watercress, washed well and spun dry
- ½ cup coarsely grated carrot

In a blender blend together oil, vinegar, 1 tablespoon walnuts, grenadine or maple syrup, and salt and pepper to taste until combined well. In a bowl toss greens, carrot, and remaining ½ tablespoon walnuts with dressing until combined well. Serves 2. May be doubled.

CURRIED COLESLAW WITH APRICOTS AND MANGO CHUTNEY

Major Grey refers to the preparation of sweet mango pickle chutney—you'll find several different brands. Remove any large chunks of mango and gingerroot and chop before using it in our dressing.

- ¼ cup mayonnaise
- 2 tablespoons plain yogurt
- 2 teaspoons chopped Major Grey's chutney
- 1½ teaspoons fresh lime juice
- ¾ teaspoon curry powder
- 2½ cups finely shredded green cabbage
- ¼ cup chopped dried apricots
- 1 tablespoon sliced almonds

In a bowl whisk together mayonnaise, yogurt, chutney, juice, curry powder, and salt and pepper to taste. Add cabbage and apricots and toss until combined well. Sprinkle coleslaw with almonds. Serves 2. May be doubled.

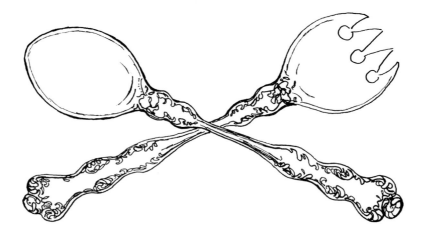

MIDDLE EASTERN PITA SALAD

In the Mediterranean region and Middle East bread salads are usually made with leftover stale bread. Here we've toasted pita pieces. If possible, use the brick-oven baked pita breads without pockets, often called "Mediterranean" pita.

½   cucumber, peeled and cut into
      ¼-inch dice
1½ 6-inch pita loaves (preferably
      Mediterranean-style, without
      pockets), cut into ¾-inch pieces
¼   cup olive oil
1   tablespoon fresh lemon juice, or
      to taste
1   garlic clove, minced
½   red bell pepper, cut into ¼-inch dice
1   vine-ripened tomato, chopped fine
¼   cup thinly sliced scallions
3   tablespoons finely chopped fresh
      mint leaves or 2 teaspoons dried
      mint, crumbled
2   tablespoons finely chopped fresh
      parsley leaves

*Garnish: inner leaves of romaine, rinsed and
spun dry, and fresh mint sprigs*

Preheat oven to 325° F.

In a sieve set over a bowl sprinkle cucumber with a pinch salt and drain 20 minutes. While cucumber is draining, in a baking pan bake pita pieces in middle of oven, shaking pan occasionally, until golden brown and crisp, about 18 minutes, and cool slightly.

Pat cucumber dry with paper towels. In a bowl whisk together oil, lemon juice, garlic, and salt and pepper to taste until combined well and stir in pita pieces, cucumber, and all remaining ingredients.

Season salad with salt and pepper and toss until combined well.

Garnish salad with romaine and mint sprigs. Serves 2. May be doubled.
Photo opposite

CELERY AND APPLE SALAD DIJON

For crisp, tart red apples choose Cortlands, Winesaps, or Northern Spies. Galas, which are yellow tinged with red, are another good choice.

2   tablespoons mayonnaise
1   tablespoon Dijon mustard
1   teaspoon cider vinegar
¼   teaspoon sugar
1   teaspoon minced fresh tarragon
      leaves or ¼ teaspoon dried tarragon,
      crumbled
1   tart apple
4   celery ribs, cut into matchsticks

Garnish: celery leaves

In a bowl whisk together mayonnaise, mustard, vinegar, sugar, tarragon, and salt and pepper to taste until smooth.

Cut and core apple. Cut apple into matchsticks and toss with celery and dressing until combined well.

Garnish salad with celery leaves. Serves 2. May be doubled.
Photo on page 113

Middle Eastern Pita Salad

SWEET POTATO AND CELERY SALAD

¾ pound sweet potato, peeled and cut
   into ½-inch cubes (about 1 large)
1 tablespoon white-wine vinegar
1½ tablespoons Dijon mustard
¼ cup vegetable oil
1 cup thinly sliced celery
¼ cup thinly sliced red bell pepper
¼ cup thinly sliced scallions
   green-leaf lettuce for lining plates

In a steamer rack set in a saucepan of boiling water steam sweet potato, covered, until tender, about 6 minutes. Transfer sweet potato to a bowl and cool. In a small bowl whisk together vinegar and mustard and add oil in a stream, whisking until emulsified. To sweet potato add dressing, celery, bell pepper, scallions, and salt and black pepper to taste and toss until combined well.

Line 2 plates with lettuce and mound sweet potato salad on top. Serves 2. May be doubled.

Photo opposite

GAZPACHO SALAD

1 vine-ripened tomato, halved,
   seeded, and cut into 1-inch chunks
1 small cucumber, peeled, halved,
   seeded, and cut into ½-inch-thick
   slices
½ red or yellow bell pepper, coarsely
   chopped
2 tablespoons thinly sliced scallion
2 tablespoons minced fresh parsley
   leaves

1 small garlic clove, minced
2 tablespoons olive oil
2 teaspoons red-wine vinegar
½ teaspoon sugar
½ cup packaged croutons, lightly
   crushed

In a bowl toss together all ingredients except croutons. Add croutons and toss until combined well. Serves 2. May be doubled.

MIXED GREENS WITH APRICOT GINGER DRESSING

Any mix of tender lettuces such as Bibb, Boston, mâche, lollo rossa, or oak-leaf lettuce can be used here. Or, for an even quicker salad, buy mesclun, a mixture of delicate young greens, available at specialty foods shops and many supermarkets.

1½ tablespoons apricot preserves
1 tablespoon soy sauce
1 tablespoon cider vinegar
1 tablespoon chopped shallot
1 teaspoon grated peeled fresh
   gingerroot
4 cups mixed lettuces

In a blender or small food processor blend preserves, soy sauce, vinegar, shallot, and gingerroot until smooth. In a bowl toss lettuces with dressing and salt and pepper to taste and serve immediately. Serves 2. May be doubled.

Each serving: 72 calories, 0 grams fat
(0% of calories from fat)

LENTIL SALAD WITH OLIVES, CAPERS, AND TOMATOES

Lentils don't need soaking and plump up nicely during a 20 minute simmer. The small, round, French lentilles du Puy, sometimes called green lentils, hold their shape well when cooked, making them an excellent choice for our salad. However, any variety, except red ones, will do.

½ cup dried lentils, picked over and rinsed

2 cups water

1½ tablespoons extra-virgin olive oil

1½ tablespoons fresh lemon juice

1 teaspoon anchovy paste

1 teaspoon Dijon mustard

½ teaspoon minced garlic

½ cup chopped seeded plum tomatoes

½ cup packed trimmed watercress, washed well, spun dry, and chopped

¼ cup black olives, pitted and chopped

1 tablespoon drained capers

In a saucepan simmer lentils in water, covered, 20 minutes, or until just tender, and drain. In a bowl whisk together oil, lemon juice, anchovy paste, mustard, and garlic until emulsified. Add lentils, remaining ingredients, and salt and pepper to taste and toss until combined well. Serves 2. May be doubled.

WATERCRESS, APPLE, AND DATE SALAD

Dates, classified as soft or semidry according to their texture, are considered a fresh fruit since they aren't dried once picked. The Deglet Noor, a semidry date, is the most common, but try plump, soft Medjools, if you can find them. They are often available at Middle Eastern markets.

1 tablespoon Sherry vinegar or red-wine vinegar

1 tablespoon fresh orange juice

1 teaspoon vegetable oil

½ teaspoon Dijon mustard

½ teaspoon sugar

½ cup dates, pitted and sliced

1 MacIntosh or Gala apple

1 Granny Smith apple

1 cup packed trimmed watercress, washed well and spun dry

In a bowl whisk together vinegar, juice, oil, mustard, sugar, and salt and pepper to taste until combined well and stir in dates. Cut and core apples. Cut apples into ½-inch pieces and toss with watercress and date mixture until combined well. Serve immediately. Serves 2. May be doubled.

Each serving: 225 calories, 3 grams fat (12% of calories from fat)

RED POTATO SALAD WITH LEMON SCALLION DRESSING

1 pound small red potatoes, cut into
  1-inch pieces
5 scallions, cut into 1-inch pieces plus
  1 coarsely chopped scallion
1½ tablespoons fresh lemon juice
2 tablespoons coarsely chopped fresh
  parsley leaves

In a saucepan cover potatoes and scallion pieces with cold salted water and bring to a boil. Simmer until potatoes are just tender, 7 to 10 minutes.

With a slotted spoon transfer cooked scallions to a blender. Drain potatoes and rinse under cold water to stop cooking. Drain potatoes well and transfer to a bowl. To cooked scallions add chopped scallion, lemon juice, and parsley and blend until smooth. Toss potatoes with dressing and season with salt and pepper. Serves 2. May be doubled.

Each serving: 203 calories, 1 gram fat
(4% of calories from fat)

CHICK-PEA, FETA, AND PARSLEY SALAD

Chick-peas, also known as garbanzos or ceci, are actually beans. Rinse them well in a sieve, then pull off and discard any loose skins.

1 16- to 19-ounce can chick-peas,
  rinsed and drained (about 2 cups)

⅓ cup crumbled feta (about 2 ounces)
½ small red onion, diced
¼ cup loosely packed fresh flat-leafed
  parsley leaves, washed well and
  spun dry
2 tablespoons olive oil (preferably
  extra-virgin)
1 tablespoon fresh orange juice, or to
  taste
1 tablespoon red-wine vinegar
1 teaspoon chopped fresh rosemary
  leaves or ½ teaspoon dried
  rosemary, crumbled
½ teaspoon ground cumin

In a large bowl toss ingredients together with salt and pepper to taste. Serves 2. May be doubled.

CHICK-PEAS AND OLIVES VINAIGRETTE

1 tablespoon olive oil
1 teaspoon white-wine vinegar
1 teaspoon Dijon mustard
1 16- to 19-ounce can chick-peas,
  rinsed and drained
1 3-ounce jar pimiento-stuffed olives
  (about ½ cup), drained and sliced
1 tablespoon minced fresh parsley
  leaves

In a bowl whisk together oil, vinegar, and mustard. Add chick-peas, olives, parsley, and salt and pepper to taste and toss until combined well. Serves 2. May be doubled.

Photo on page 120

Plum and Apricot Puff Pastry Tarts

Frozen puff pastry sheets help you make truly elegant desserts in a snap. Look for the Pepperidge Farm brand, available in the freezer case of many supermarkets. And, since fully ripe fresh apricots are difficult to find outside of California markets, feel free to substitute one ripe nectarine or peach.

1 1-inch piece vanilla bean, split lengthwise
1 tablespoon sugar
1 pinch cinnamon
1 ½-pound frozen puff pastry sheet, thawed
2 plums, cut into ¼-inch-thick slices
2 fresh apricots, cut into ¼-inch-thick slices
3 tablespoons apricot jam

Accompaniment: vanilla ice cream

Preheat oven to 400° F.

Scrape seeds from vanilla bean with a knife into a small bowl, discarding pod, and stir in sugar and cinnamon.

On a lightly floured surface roll out pastry about ⅛ inch thick and cut out two 6- by 5½-inch rectangles. Arrange pastry on a baking sheet and fold edges in on all sides to form ½-inch borders, leaving corners unfolded. Pinch corners to form points and twist. Press points gently onto baking sheet. On pastry arrange plum and apricot slices in rows, overlapping them slightly, and sprinkle with sugar mixture.

Bake tarts in middle of oven until pastry is golden brown, 20 to 25 minutes. While tarts are baking, in a small saucepan heat jam over low heat, stirring, until melted and strain through a sieve into a cup. On a rack cool tarts slightly and brush with jam.

Serve tarts warm with ice cream. Makes 2 individual tarts. May be doubled.

Photo opposite

Plum and Apricot Puff Pastry Tart

PINEAPPLE UPSIDE-DOWN CARROT CAKES

  3 tablespoons unsalted butter, softened
  2 tablespoons firmly packed brown sugar
  ½ cup canned pineapple chunks, drained
  ¼ cup all-purpose flour
  ¼ teaspoon baking powder
  ¼ teaspoon cinnamon
  ⅛ teaspoon ground ginger
  3 tablespoons granulated sugar
  1 large egg
  ¼ teaspoon vanilla
  2 tablespoons finely shredded carrot

Preheat oven to 350° F.

In a small saucepan melt 2 tablespoons butter and divide between two 1-cup ramekins. Sprinkle brown sugar over butter. Pat pineapple dry and arrange in bottom of ramekins, pressing lightly to fit.

In a small bowl whisk together flour, baking powder, cinnamon, ginger, and a pinch salt. In a bowl with an electric mixer beat together remaining tablespoon butter and granulated sugar until combined well. Beat in egg and vanilla until combined and beat in flour mixture and carrot until batter is just combined.

Divide batter between ramekins and put on a baking sheet. Bake cakes in middle of oven until a tester comes out clean, about 20 minutes. Run a thin knife around edge of each ramekin and invert cakes onto plates. Makes 2 individual cakes. May be doubled.

ANGEL FOOD CAKE ORANGE TRIFLES

Here we urge you to take a shortcut—use a store-bought angel food cake. You only need a small piece and no one will ever know the difference!

  1 tablespoon sugar
  ¼ teaspoon cornstarch
  1 large egg
  1 tablespoon sweet orange marmalade
  ¾ cup skim milk
  1½ cups ½-inch cubes angel food cake
  ¾ cup ½-inch pieces of orange, membranes discarded

In a bowl whisk together sugar, cornstarch, and a pinch salt and whisk in egg and marmalade. In a 1½- to 2-quart heavy saucepan bring milk just to a boil. Add hot milk in a stream to egg mixture, whisking, and transfer to saucepan. Bring custard to a boil over moderate heat, whisking constantly, and simmer, whisking, 1 minute. Transfer custard to a metal bowl set in a larger bowl of ice and cold water, and let stand, stirring occasionally, until cool.

In a bowl toss together cake and orange and divide between 2 stemmed glasses. Spoon custard over cake mixture and serve immediately. Serves 2. May be doubled.

Each serving: 225 calories, 3 grams fat (12% of calories from fat)

Individual Chocolate Soufflés

¼ cup sugar plus additional for
   coating gratin dishes
2 tablespoons all-purpose flour
2 tablespoons Dutch-process cocoa
   powder
1 tablespoon cold unsalted butter
½ cup milk
½ ounce unsweetened chocolate,
   chopped fine
1 large egg yolk
2 large egg whites

Garnish: confectioners' sugar

Preheat oven to 400° F. Butter two ¾-cup gratin dishes and coat with additional sugar, shaking out excess sugar.

In a small bowl blend together 2 tablespoons sugar, flour, cocoa powder, butter, and a pinch salt until mixture resembles meal. In a small heavy saucepan bring milk just to a boil and whisk in cocoa mixture and chocolate. Cook mixture over moderate heat, whisking, until thickened, about 15 seconds and cool 30 seconds.

In a bowl whisk yolk lightly and whisk in about 1 tablespoon chocolate mixture. Whisk in remaining chocolate mixture. In another bowl whisk whites with a pinch salt until they hold soft peaks and whisk in remaining 2 tablespoons sugar, a little at a time, until meringue holds stiff peaks. Stir one fourth of meringue into chocolate mixture to lighten and fold in remaining meringue gently but thoroughly.

Divide soufflé batter between gratin dishes and put on a baking sheet. Bake chocolate soufflés in middle of oven 15 minutes, or until puffed.

Dust soufflés with confectioners' sugar and serve immediately. Serves 2. May be doubled.

Photo on page 8

Deep-Dish Apple Pies

2 MacIntosh apples (about ¾ pound)
1 teaspoon fresh lemon juice
2 tablespoons plus 1 teaspoon sugar
1 teaspoon all-purpose flour
¼ teaspoon cinnamon
⅛ teaspoon nutmeg
1 packaged pie dough round

Preheat oven to 400° F.

Peel and core apples. Cut apples into 1-inch pieces and in a bowl toss together with juice, 2 tablespoons sugar, flour, spices, and a pinch salt. Divide filling between two 1-cup ramekins, mounding it.

Cut two 6-inch rounds from pie dough. Drape rounds over filling and press edge to inside of ramekins, crimping dough. Brush dough with water and sprinkle with remaining teaspoon sugar.

Cut a 1-inch vent in each crust with a sharp knife and bake pies in middle of oven until filling bubbles and crust is golden, about 30 minutes. Makes 2 individual pies. May be doubled.

BITTERSWEET CHOCOLATE FALLEN SOUFFLÉ CAKES

>   sugar for coating ramekins
> 6 ounces fine-quality bittersweet chocolate (not unsweetened), chopped
> 1½ tablespoons unsalted butter
> 2 teaspoons instant espresso powder dissolved in 1 tablespoon hot water
> 2 tablespoons Kahlúa or dark rum
> 2 large egg yolks
> 3 large egg whites
> 3 tablespoons heavy cream

Garnish: grated bittersweet chocolate

Accompaniment: lightly sweetened whipped cream

Preheat oven to 375° F. Butter two 1¼-cup ramekins and coat with sugar, knocking out excess sugar.

In a small metal bowl set over a small saucepan of barely simmering water melt 4 ounces chocolate and 1 tablespoon butter with espresso mixture and 1 tablespoon Kahlúa or rum and whisk until smooth. Remove bowl from heat and cool chocolate mixture 5 minutes. Whisk in yolks, 1 at a time. In a bowl with an electric mixer beat whites with a pinch salt until they just hold stiff peaks. Stir about one fourth whites into chocolate mixture to lighten and fold in remaining whites gently but thoroughly.

Divide batter between ramekins. Bake cakes in middle of oven 17 to 20 minutes, or until puffed and a tester comes out almost clean.

While cakes are baking, in another small metal bowl set over pan of barely simmering water melt remaining 2 ounces chocolate with remaining ½ tablespoon butter and heavy cream and whisk until smooth. Remove bowl from heat and whisk in remaining tablespoon Kahlúa or rum.

Cool cakes in ramekins on a rack 3 minutes. Pour sauce onto 2 plates. Run a thin knife around edge of each ramekin and invert cakes onto plates. Top cakes with whipped cream and garnish with grated chocolate. Serves 2. May be doubled.

Photo opposite

PEACH AND APRICOT CRISP

> 1 16-ounce can sliced peaches, drained
> ¼ cup quick-cooking rolled oats
> 3 tablespoons chopped almonds
> 2 tablespoons cold unsalted butter
> 2 tablespoons all-purpose flour
> 2 tablespoons firmly packed light brown sugar
> ⅛ teaspoon almond extract
> 2 tablespoons chopped dried apricots
> 1 tablespoon peach schnapps

Preheat oven to 450° F. and butter a 2-cup shallow baking dish.

Drain peaches in one layer on paper towels.

In a small bowl blend oats, almonds, butter, flour, brown sugar, extract, and a pinch salt until mixture resembles coarse meal. In baking dish toss together peaches, apricots, and schnapps and sprinkle oat mixture over fruit.

Bake crisp in middle of oven 15 minutes, or until top is crisp and golden. Serves 2. May be doubled.

ORANGE COCONUT CUPCAKES

2½ tablespoons unsalted butter,
    softened
⅓ cup sugar
1 large egg
3 tablespoons fresh orange juice
1 tablespoon bourbon
¼ teaspoon vanilla
½ cup all-purpose flour
1 teaspoon baking powder
¼ cup sweetened flaked coconut

Preheat oven to 350° F. and line six ½-cup muffin tins with paper liners.

In a bowl with an electric mixer beat together butter and sugar until light and fluffy. Beat in egg until combined well and beat in juice, bourbon, and vanilla. Into egg mixture sift together flour, baking powder, and a pinch salt. Beat batter on low speed until just combined and stir in coconut.

Divide batter among paper-lined tins and bake in middle of oven 15 minutes, or until a tester comes out clean. Transfer cupcakes to a rack and cool 5 minutes. Makes 6 cupcakes.

ALMOND COOKIE CRISPS

For thin, dainty crisps don't be tempted to drop larger than 1 teaspoon measures of batter onto parchment-lined baking sheets, and space them out without crowding. Use a fork to spread this batter very, very thinly into 2-inch rounds.

1 large egg white
¼ cup superfine sugar
1 teaspoon unsalted butter, melted
    and cooled
3 drops almond extract
3 tablespoons sliced almonds
1 tablespoon all-purpose flour

Preheat oven to 350° F. Lightly grease 2 baking sheets and line with parchment paper.

In a bowl beat white until frothy and beat in sugar, butter, extract, and a pinch salt. Stir in almonds and flour until batter is just combined. Drop batter by teaspoons 3 inches apart onto baking sheets, spreading batter with back of a fork into 2-inch rounds.

Bake cookies in 2 batches in middle of oven until golden, about 8 minutes, and transfer on parchment paper to racks. Cool cookies completely and carefully peel off paper. Makes about 12 cookies. May be doubled.

Each cookie: 34 calories, 1 gram fat
(26% of calories from fat)

POACHED SPICED APPLE WITH LEMON YOGURT SAUCE

  ¾ cup water
  1½ tablespoons sugar
  1 tablespoon rum
  1 large pinch cinnamon
  1 pinch nutmeg
  1 Granny Smith apple
  1½ teaspoons fresh lemon juice
  1½ tablespoons honey
  ½ cup plain low-fat yogurt

In a heavy 1½- to 2-quart saucepan bring water, sugar, rum, spices, and a pinch salt to a boil, stirring until sugar is dissolved, and simmer syrup 5 minutes. Peel and core apple. Cut apple into ¼-inch-thick slices and poach in syrup, covered, until tender, about 15 minutes. Transfer apple with a slotted spoon to a metal bowl and boil syrup until reduced to about 3 tablespoons. Pour syrup over apple. Set bowl in a larger bowl of ice and cold water and let mixture stand, stirring occasionally, until slightly cooled. In a small bowl whisk together juice and honey until honey is dissolved and whisk in yogurt.

Serve apple mixture topped with yogurt sauce. Serves 2. May be doubled.

Each serving: 176 calories, 1 gram fat (5% of calories from fat)

CHOCOLATE KAHLÚA BAVARIAN

For best results when whipping cream, chill your bowl and beaters in the freezer for 30 minutes beforehand, and use very cold cream.

  ½ teaspoon unflavored gelatin
  1 tablespoon cold water
  2 tablespoons granulated sugar
  1 cup well-chilled heavy cream
  2 ounces fine-quality bittersweet chocolate (not unsweetened), chopped fine
  2 tablespoons Kahlúa
  1 tablespoon confectioners' sugar

In a very small saucepan sprinkle gelatin over cold water and let soften 1 minute. Heat mixture over moderate heat, stirring, until gelatin is dissolved. Stir in granulated sugar and ¼ cup cream and bring just to a boil, stirring until sugar is dissolved. Remove pan from heat and stir in chocolate and Kahlúa until chocolate is melted. Transfer mixture to a metal bowl set in a larger bowl of ice and cold water and stir until cold and thickened. In a bowl beat remaining ¾ cup cream with confectioners' sugar until it just holds stiff peaks and fold into chocolate mixture gently but thoroughly.

Spoon Bavarian into 2 stemmed glasses and chill at least 15 minutes, or until ready to serve. Serves 2. May be doubled.

PLUM PARFAITS

Plums are found in many varieties and range in flavor from sweet to tart. For our purée, feel free to choose different kinds for a range of flavor.

    3 plums, cut into 1-inch pieces
   ¼ cup plus 2 tablespoons cold water
    3 tablespoons Ruby Port
    3 tablespoons plus 2 teaspoons sugar
    1 tablespoon fresh lemon juice
    2 teaspoons unflavored gelatin
   ⅓ cup well-chilled heavy cream

In a small saucepan stir together plums, reserving a few pieces for garnish, ¼ cup water, Port, 3 tablespoons sugar, and lemon juice and simmer, covered, 10 minutes, or until plums are tender. In a cup sprinkle gelatin over remaining 2 tablespoons water and let soften 1 minute. In a blender purée hot plum mixture with gelatin mixture until smooth. Transfer purée to a metal bowl set in a larger bowl of ice and cold water and chill, stirring frequently, until thickened to consistency of applesauce. While purée is chilling, in a small bowl beat cream with remaining 2 teaspoons sugar until it just holds stiff peaks and reserve about 2 tablespoons whipped cream for garnish.

    In 2 stemmed glasses layer remaining whipped cream and plum purée, alternating them. Mix layers together slightly by drawing handle of a spoon from bottom up sides of glasses a few times.

    Garnish each parfait with a dollop of reserved whipped cream. Slice reserved plum pieces and arrange on top. Chill parfaits at least 15 minutes, or until ready to serve. Serves 2. May be doubled.

    Photo opposite

BERRY AND GINGER SOUR CREAM BRÛLÉE

In this mock crème brûlée the fruit is topped with a no-cook sour cream, ginger, and vanilla sauce instead of a custard, making this a super-quick dish to assemble and broil.

    2 cups picked-over mixed fruit such as blueberries, raspberries, halved strawberries, and seedless grapes
   ½ cup sour cream
    1 teaspoon finely chopped crystallized ginger
   ½ teaspoon vanilla
    3 tablespoons firmly packed light brown sugar

Preheat broiler.

    In a small gratin or other shallow flame-proof baking dish arrange fruit in one layer. In a small bowl stir together sour cream, ginger, and vanilla and drop in dollops on top of fruit, spreading to cover fruit completely. Rub brown sugar through a sieve evenly over topping and broil about 3 inches from heat 2 minutes, or until brown sugar is melted. Serves 2. May be doubled.

RASPBERRY MINT SORBET

Using frozen raspberries speeds up making this frosty treat. Simply break apart packaged raspberries and purée them with the syrup. You won't even need an ice-cream maker to freeze the sorbet.

- ½ cup water
- 2 tablespoons dark rum
- 2 tablespoons sugar
- 1 cup fresh mint leaves, rinsed and spun dry
- 1 10-ounce package frozen raspberries in syrup

Garnish: fresh mint sprigs

In a 1½- to 2-quart saucepan bring water, rum, and sugar to a boil, stirring until sugar is dissolved and remove pan from heat. Add mint and steep 5 minutes. Strain mixture through a sieve, pressing hard on mint, into a small metal bowl set in a larger bowl of ice and cold water and stir until cold. In a blender blend mint syrup and frozen raspberries until smooth, stirring as necessary to blend berries, and spread in a metal ice tray (without dividers) or small baking pan. Freeze sorbet, covered with plastic wrap, at least 20 minutes, or until ready to serve.

Spoon sorbet into stemmed glasses and garnish with mint sprigs. Serves 2. May be doubled.

Each serving: 249 calories, 1 gram fat (4% of calories from fat)

STRAWBERRY BANANA FOOL

If ripe, sweet strawberries are out of season, feel free to substitute frozen (not in syrup). Partially thaw them and drain the excess juice. Bananas may be used to garnish the top.

½ cup sliced fresh strawberries
2 tablespoons firmly packed brown sugar
1 teaspoon fresh lemon juice
½ cup sliced ripe banana (about 1)
½ cup well-chilled heavy cream
¼ teaspoon vanilla

Garnish: about ¼ cup sliced fresh strawberries

In a heavy saucepan simmer strawberries, brown sugar, lemon juice, and a pinch salt, stirring, 5 minutes. In a blender or food processor purée strawberry mixture and banana. Transfer purée to a metal bowl set in a larger bowl of ice and cold water and stir until very cold. In another bowl combine cream and vanilla and set bowl in larger bowl of ice water. Beat cream until it just holds stiff peaks and fold into purée until just combined. Spoon fool into 2 stemmed glasses and chill at least 15 minutes, or until ready to serve.

Garnish fool with sliced strawberries. Serves 2. May be doubled.

TIRAMISÙ CHOCOLATE WAFER CAKE

Mascarpone, the velvety smooth, fresh cheese from northern Italy, adds creamy sweet flavor to our chocolate cream. Cream cheese will also do the job, but it is less sweet and more dense in texture.

2 tablespoons *mascarpone* cheese or softened cream cheese
1 tablespoon sugar
⅓ cup well-chilled heavy cream
1 tablespoon grated semisweet chocolate
2 teaspoons strong brewed coffee
2 teaspoons rum or coffee liqueur
5 Nabisco chocolate wafers

In a bowl with a mixer beat *mascarpone* and sugar until smooth. Add cream and chocolate and beat until mixture holds stiff peaks. In a small bowl stir together coffee and rum (or liqueur) and brush onto wafers.

Sandwich wafers together to form a tower using about two-thirds cream mixture. On a plate arrange tower on its side and spread remaining cream over it. Chill cake, loosely covered, 30 minutes. With a sharp knife halve cake diagonally. Serves 2. May be doubled to make 2 cakes.

Index

Page numbers in *italics* indicate color photographs
🍂 indicates recipes that are leaner/lighter

B

D

FLOUNDER, with Sesame Seed Crust,
   Fried, Cucumber Salad and, 82
FOOL
   Caramel Pear, 47
   Strawberry Banana, 181
FRITTATA, Pepperoni Pizza, 132
FRITTERS, Sweet-Potato Bacon,
   130, *131*
FROZEN DESSERTS
   Sorbet, Raspberry Mint, 180
   Yogurt with Raspberry Port Sauce, 15
FRUIT. *See* names of fruits
FRUIT DESSERTS
   Apple Pies, Deep-Dish, 173
   Apple, Poached Spiced, with Lemon
      Yogurt Sauce, 177
   Berry and Ginger Sour Cream Brûlée,
      178
   Fool, Caramel Pear, 47
   Fool, Strawberry Banana, 181
   Fresh Fruit, Almond Galette with
      Whipped Cream and, 43
   Peach and Apricot Crisp, 175
   Pears, Spiced Poached, *48*, 51
   Plum and Apricot Tarts, Puff Pastry,
      170, 171
   Plum Parfaits, 178, *179*

G

GALETTE, Almond, with Fresh Fruit and
   Whipped Cream, 43
GARLIC
   Black Bean and Rice Soup with, 68
   Bread, 19
   Chicken Cutlets with Ginger, Scallion
      and, 118
   Mahimahi, Grilled, with Lime, Cumin
      and, 82
   Spinach with Ginger and, Stir-Fried,
      109, 159

Yogurt Grilled Okra, 157
GAZPACHO
   Citrus, 73
   Salad, 166
GINGER(ED)
   Broth, Red Snapper, Pan-Seared, in,
      40, 42
   Chicken Cutlets with Scallion, Garlic
      and, 118
   Dressing, Apricot, with Mixed
      Greens, 166
   Dressing, Lime, with Avocado and
      Hearts of Palm Salad, 162
   Maple Syrup, Pear Pancake, Baked,
      with, 125, *127*
   Red Snapper, Whole, with Shiitake
      Mushrooms, 83
   Sour Cream Brûlée, Berry and, 178
   Spinach, with Garlic and, Stir-Fried,
      109, 159
   Waffles, Banana, 128
GOAT CHEESE, and Sun-Dried Tomato
   Quesadillas, 60
GORGONZOLA
   Ravioli, with Roasted Pepper Pesto,
      144
   Soufflé, Scallion and, 133
GOULASH, Beef, with Red Bell Peppers,
      106
GRANOLA Muffins, 129
GRAPEFRUIT, Beet, and Blue Cheese
      Salad, *160*, 161
GRAPES, Chicken and Shallots with
      Riesling and, 115
GRATIN
   Potato, Gruyère, *109*, 155
   Summer Squash and Tomato,
      ·Provençal-Style, 159
GREEN BEANS, Spicy Sautéed, with
      Bacon, 150
GREENS. *See also* names of greens
   Mixed, with Apricot Ginger Dressing,
      166

Table Setting Acknowledgments

Any items in the photographs not credited are privately owned. All addresses are in New York City unless otherwise indicated.

JACKET

Jamaican-Spiced Pork Tenderloin; Sweet Potato Purée; Black Bean and Roasted Vegetable Salad (front): Deruta hand-painted ceramic dinnerplate designed by Jane Axel; "Zig Zag" stainless steel knife and fork designed by Lisa Jenks—Avventura, 463 Amsterdam Avenue.

Spiced Poached Pear (back): Dartington glass bowl; Carlo Moretti Champagne flute (from a set of six designs)—Avventura, 463 Amsterdam Avenue. "Palladio" ceramic and gold-leaf dessert plate; "Cherub Face" candle—Vietri, (800) 277-5933 for list of stores. Gold- and silver-leaf background—Richard Pellicci, (914) 271-6710.

INTRODUCTION

Individual Chocolate Soufflés (page 8): French faience salad plates (from a set of 4 plates and a compote), circa 1900—Barneys New York, Seventh Avenue and 17th Street. Scottish nineteenth-century sterling flat-ware—F. Gorevic & Sons, Inc., 635 Madison Avenue. Majolica pitcher, circa 1870—Kentshire Antiques, Bergdorf Goodman, 754 Fifth Avenue. Table covering is "Minton"

fabric designed by Pierre Frey (available through decorator)—Brunschwig & Fils, Inc., 979 Third Avenue.

MENUS

Menu Opener

Chilled Avocado Soup with Chili Coriander Cream (pages 10 and 11): Gien "Tamarin" faience plates—Baccarat, 625 Madison Avenue. "Bamboo" sterling flatware—Tiffany & Co., 727 Fifth Avenue. "Laurel Green" wineglasses and water goblets—for stores call Sasaki (212) 686-5080. "Palma" cotton fabric (available through decorator)—Brunschwig & Fils, Inc., 979 Third Avenue.

An Alfresco Spring Brunch

Spinach, Red Pepper, and Feta Quiche; Romaine Salad with Radishes, Olives, and Mint (page 12): Limoges dinner plate designed by Hilton McConnico; Retroneau stainless-steel knife and fork; Smyers wineglass—Bergdorf Goodman, 754 Fifth Avenue.

Carefree Pasta Lunch

Pasta with Prosciutto, Peppers, and Herbs (page 16): Ceramic bowls; Le Jacquard Français cotton napkin—Wolfman • Gold & Good Company, 117 Mercer Street.

Lunch by the Fire
Leek, Potato, and Sausage Soup (page 20): All items in the photograph are privately owned.

A Lazy Day Summer Lunch
Steak Salad with Pickled Vegetables (page 24): Hand-sponged stoneware dinner plate with porcelain overlay from the Ellen Evans Collection for Terrafirma—for retail stores contact Terrafirma, 152 West 25th Street, tel. (212) 645-7600. Hammered bronze flatware—Zona, 97 Greene Street.

Barbecue for a Special Occasion
Swordfish, Bacon, and Cherry Tomato Kebabs; Sautéed Spinach Chiffonade with Shallots (page 28): Ceramic dinner plate, glass tumbler, straw place mat, and cotton napkin—Ad Hoc Softwares, 410 West Broadway.

A Festive Summer Dinner
Vegetable Tortilla Lasagne (page 32): Ceramic plate; "Harlequin" stainless-steel flatware designed by Lisa Jenks; linen napkin; jute place mat—Wolfman • Gold & Good Company, 117 Mercer Street.

A Hearty Bachelor's Dinner
Steak au Poivre; Spinach with Pernod; Turnips with Bread Crumbs and Parsley (page 36): Ceramic plate—Fishs Eddy, 889 Broadway. Au Nain stainless-steel steak knife with rosewood handle; wineglass—Bridge Kitchenware Corporation, 214 East 52nd Street, tel. (800) 274-3435.

An Elegant Asian Dinner
Pan-Seared Red Snapper in Ginger Broth (page 40): Crystal bowl designed by Elsa Peretti—Tiffany & Co., 727 Fifth Avenue. Sasaki "Astrakan" dinner plate designed by Carin Colombo; Sasaki "Asana" stainless-steel soup spoon; Calypso wineglass; cotton napkin; bamboo tray—Frank McIntosh Home Collection at Henri Bendel, 712 Fifth Avenue.

Dinner for a Snowy Eve
Butternut Squash and Apple Soup with Bacon; Cheddar Chutney Toasts (page 44): Mottahedeh "Palace Blue" china—Cardel, Ltd., 621 Madison Avenue. "Les Feuilles" linen and cotton fabric (available through decorator)—Grey Watkins, 979 Third Avenue.

Maharajah's Supper
Spiced Poached Pear (page 48): See credits for back jacket.

RECIPE OPENER
Chilled Avocado Soup with Coriander Chili Cream (pages 54 and 55): All items in photograph are privately owned.

STARTERS
Noodles and Smoked Salmon with Dill Sauce (page 56): "Marbleized" porcelain plate—Villeroy & Boch Creations, 974 Madison Avenue. Val St. Lambert "Laeken" wineglass—Cardel, Ltd., 621 Madison Avenue.

Yellow Tomato Salad with Lemongrass (page 59): "Mosaic" Italian ceramic salad plate—Zona, 97 Greene Street. "Fiddlehead" stainless-steel flatware—Pottery Barn, 117 East 59th Street. Italian linen napkins—Frank McIntosh Home Collection at Henri Bendel, 712 Fifth Avenue.

Radishes with Chive Butter (page 62): Victorian silver-plate salver—S. Wyler Inc., 941 Lexington Avenue.

SOUPS

New England Clam Chowder (page 66): All items in photograph are privately owned.

Winter Vegetable Soup (page 71): Italian alder wood soup bowl and plate by Daniela Mola—Zona, 97 Greene Street. Turkish handwoven cotton throw—Turquerie, (212) 421-5429 for list of stores.

Chilled Zucchini Soup (page 73): Italian earthenware soup plate and under-plate; acrylic-handled soup spoon; hand-stitched linen napkin—Wolfman • Gold & Good Company, 117 Mercer Street.

FISH

Salmon Teriyaki with Carrots and Onions (page 76): Porcelain dinner plate and ceramic square plate; lacquered chopsticks; linen napkin; porcelain teapot; bamboo trivet; ceramic tea cup—Takashimaya, 693 Fifth Avenue.

Norwegian-Style Poached Salmon with Anchovy Butter; Rice with Kale and Tomatoes (page 81): "Blue Pheasant" porcelain dinner plates; "Palm" hand-painted crystal wineglasses designed by Ken Done for Kosta Boda—Royal Copenhagen Porcelain/Georg Jensen Silversmiths, 683 Madison Avenue.

Sole with Citrus and Olive Sauce; Lima Bean Purée with Olive Oil and Oregano (page 84): "Francescano" majolica dinner plate designed by Frank Termini for Deruta—Deruta of Italy, (212) 686-0808. "Lotus" crystal wineglass designed by Andrée Putman for Sasaki—Sasaki, (212) 686-5080. Indian cotton place mat and napkin—The Pottery Barn, 117 East 59th Street.

SHELLFISH

Curried Chili Shrimp with Scallion Rice (page 88): "Indian Summer" porcelain dinner plates by Taitù—Bloomingdale's, 1000 Third Avenue.

Linguine with White Clam Sauce and Tomato; Onion and Black Pepper Flatbreads (page 93): Stoneware chop plate; French acrylic and stainless-steel salad servers; cotton napkins—Wolfman • Gold & Good Company, 117 Mercer Street.

Sautéed Scallops with Watercress and Corn Salad (page 96): All items in photograph are privately owned.

MEATS

Curried Pork Chops with Brandied Peach and Crab Apple Chutney; Brussels Sprouts and Onions with Dill (page 100): Spode "Blue Geranium" Imperialware dinner plate—for information call (609) 866-2900. "Liberty" wineglass—ABC Carpet & Home, 888 Broadway.

Vietnamese-Style Grilled Steak with Noodles (page 105): "Vie Sauvage" bone china dinner plate—Villeroy & Boch Creations, 974 Madison Avenue. "Galaxy" stainless-steel flat-ware designed by Ward Bennett; "San Marino" crystal wineglass—Sasaki, (212) 686-5080.

Rack of Lamb with Caramelized Shallot and Thyme Crust; Stir-Fried Spinach with Ginger and Garlic; Gruyère Potato Gratin (page 109): Hand-painted ceramic dinner plates by Dan Bleier—Avventura, 463 Amsterdam Avenue. "Loop" hammered stainless-steel flatware and "Vesuvio" bronze votive candle holder, both by Michael Aram—Platypus, 126 Spring

Street. Wineglass by Mathias—Takashimaya, 693 Fifth Avenue. Cotton napkins by Paula Sweet—Frank McIntosh Home Collection at Henri Bendel, 712 Fifth Avenue.

POULTRY

Grilled Chicken Breasts Stuffed with Ham and Saga Blue Cheese; Celery and Apple Salad Dijon (page 112): Cassis ceramic dinner plate; Spratling sterling and ebony fork and knife; cotton napkin; jute place mat—Zona, 97 Greene Street.

Chicken and Sausage Couscous (page 117): Deshoulières "Pearls of the Orient" Limoges dinner plate—Jacques Jugeat Inc., (201) 939-4199. "Casbah" stainless-steel flatware; wineglass; and decanter—The Pottery Barn, 117 East 59th Street.

Lemon Chicken and Roasted Red Pepper Sandwiches; Chick-Peas and Olives Vinaigrette (page 120): Beer glasses—Pottery Barn, 117 East 59th Street. Cotton napkins— April Cornell, 860 Lexington Avenue.

BREAKFASTS AND BRUNCHES

Spicy Smoked Salmon Corn Cakes (page 124): La Clé des Champs faience dinner plate and cup and saucer by Gien—Baccarat, 625 Madison Avenue. Italian pewter flatware— Frank McIntosh Home Collection at Henri Bendel, 712 Fifth Avenue. Old fashioned glass—Pottery Barn, 117 East 59th Street.

Baked Pear Pancake with Gingered Maple Syrup (page 127): Le Creuset enameled cast-iron skillet with non-stick coating from

Schiller & Asmus, Inc., P. O. Box 575, Yemassee, South Carolina.

Sweet-Potato Bacon Fritters (page 131): All items in photograph are privately owned.

PASTA AND GRAINS

Artichoke and Olive Marinara Sauce (page 136): T. G. Green "Cornish Blue-Band" ceramic luncheon plate—Dean & DeLuca, Inc., 560 Broadway. "Rosso Merlino" *faux marbre* background by Richard Pellicci, (914) 271-6710.

Pasta with Uncooked Tomato and Olive Sauce (page 139): "Dit-Dash" ceramic bowl and plate by Jill Rosenwald; "Bouton d'Or" cotton napkin; mosaic tabletop (on iron base)—ABC Carpet & Home, 888 Broadway. "Sphere" bronze flatware by Izabel Lam—Platypus, 126 Spring Street. Wineglass—Wolfman • Gold & Good Company, 117 Mercer Street.

Pepperoni Spaghetti Cake (page 143): Ceramic plate; "Double Helix" stainless-steel flatware; wineglass; cotton napkin (background); painted wood tray—Frank McIntosh Home Collection at Henri Bendel, 712 Fifth Avenue.

VEGETABLES

Vegetable Stew with Couscous (page 148): French stoneware dinner plates; Ralph Lauren "Watchband" stainless-steel flatware; iittala beer steins; cotton towels; Woodnotes 79- by 35-inch wood-fiber runner—Ad Hoc Softwares, 410 West Broadway.

Black Bean Tostadas with Curly Endive Salad (page 153): Hand-blown glass plate and wineglass; handmade tin plate; Mexican handwoven cotton throw and napkin—Pan American Phoenix, 857 Lexington Avenue.

Sautéed Jerusalem Artichokes with Peppers (page 156): All items in photograph are privately owned.

SALADS

Grapefruit, Beet, and Blue Cheese Salad (page 160): Ceramic luncheon plate, service plate, and straw place mat—Frank McIntosh Home Collection at Henri Bendel, 712 Fifth Avenue.

Middle Eastern Pita Salad (page 164): Gien "Volupté" faience platter—Baccarat, 625 Madison Avenue.

Sweet Potato and Celery Salad (page 167): All items in photograph are privately owned.

DESSERTS

Plum and Apricot Puff Pastry Tart (page 170): French ceramic plate from Parasol Collections—for stores call (203) 746-8295.

Bittersweet Chocolate Fallen Soufflé Cakes (page 174): Davenport pearl ware dessert plates (from a set of 6), circa 1810— Bardith Ltd., 901 Madison Avenue. Sterling silver dessert fork and spoon, London, 1870— James II Galleries, Ltd., 11 East 57th Street.

Plum Parfaits (page 179): Hand-blown footed glasses—Bergdorf Goodman, 754 Fifth Avenue. "Wallis" stainless-steel spoons (from five-piece place settings) by Vicente Wolf for Sasaki—The L • S Collection, 765 Madison Avenue. Lacquered wood tray designed by Cynthia Carey; cotton napkin—Frank McIntosh Home Collection at Henri Bendel, 712 Fifth Avenue.

Credits